Collins

ROYAL
OBSERVATORY
GREENWICH

2021 GUIDE
to the
NIGHT SKY

Storm Dunlop and Wil Tirion

D1439860

Published by Collins
An imprint of HarperCollins Publishers
Westerhill Road
Bishopbriggs
Glasgow G64 2QT
www.harpercollins.co.uk

In association with
Royal Museums Greenwich, the group name for the National Maritime Museum,
Royal Observatory Greenwich, Queen's House and *Cutty Sark*
www.rmg.co.uk

A catalogue record for this book is available from the British Library

ISBN 978-0-00-838904-8

10 9 8 7 6 5 4 3 2 1

Printed in China by RR Donnelley APS

If you would like to comment on any aspect of this book, please contact us at the above address or online.
e-mail: collinsmaps@harpercollins.co.uk

 facebook.com/CollinsAstronomy

 @CollinsAstro

MIX
Paper from
responsible sources
FSC www.fsc.org   **FSC™ C007454**

This book is produced from independently certified
FSC™ paper to ensure responsible forest management.

For more information visit: www.harpercollins.co.uk/green

Contents

Introduction

The aim of this Guide is to help people find their way around the night sky, by showing how the stars that are visible change from month to month and by including details of various events that occur throughout the year. The objects and events described may be observed with the naked eye, or nothing more complicated than a pair of binoculars.

The conditions for observing naturally vary over the course of the year. During the summer, twilight may persist throughout the night and make it difficult to see the faintest stars. There are three recognized stages of twilight: civil twilight, when the Sun is less than 6° below the horizon; nautical twilight, when the Sun is between 6° and 12° below the horizon; and astronomical twilight, when the Sun is between 12° and 18° below the horizon. Full darkness occurs only when the Sun is more than 18° below the horizon. During nautical twilight, only the very brightest stars are visible. During astronomical twilight, the faintest stars visible to the naked eye may be seen directly overhead, but are lost at lower altitudes. As the diagram shows, during June and most of July full darkness never occurs at the latitude of London, and at Edinburgh nautical twilight persists throughout the whole night, so at that latitude only the very brightest stars are visible.

Another factor that affects the visibility of objects is the amount of moonlight in the sky. At Full Moon, it may be very difficult to see some of the fainter stars and objects, and even when the Moon is at a smaller phase it may seriously interfere with visibility if it is near the stars or planets in which you are interested. A full lunar calendar is given for each month and may be used to see when nights are likely to be darkest and best for observation.

The celestial sphere

All the objects in the sky (including the Sun, Moon and stars) appear to lie at some indeterminate distance on a large sphere, centred on the Earth. This **celestial sphere** has various reference points and features that are related to those of the Earth. If the Earth's rotational axis is extended, for example, it points to the North and South Celestial Poles, which are thus in line with the North and South Poles on Earth. Similarly, the **celestial**

The duration of twilight throughout the year at London and Edinburgh.

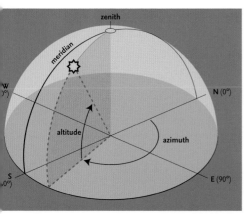

Measuring altitude and azimuth on the celestial sphere.

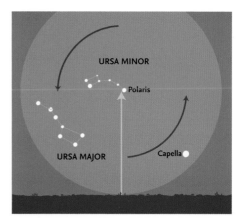

The altitude of the North Celestial Pole equals the observer's latitude.

equator lies in the same plane as the Earth's equator, and divides the sky into northern and southern hemispheres. Because this Guide is written for use in Britain and Ireland, the area of the sky that it describes includes the whole of the northern celestial hemisphere and those portions of the southern that become visible at different times of the year. Stars in the far south, however, remain invisible throughout the year, and are not included.

It is useful to know some of the special terms for various parts of the sky. As seen by an observer, half of the celestial sphere is invisible, below the horizon. The point directly overhead is known as the **zenith**, and the (invisible) one below one's feet as the **nadir**. The line running from the north point on the horizon, up through the zenith and then down to the south point is the **meridian**. This is an important invisible line in the sky, because objects are highest in the sky, and thus easiest to see, when they cross the meridian in the south. Objects are said to **transit**, when they cross this line in the sky.

In this book, reference is frequently made in the text and in the diagrams to the standard compass points around the horizon. The position of any object in the sky may be described by its **altitude** (measured in degrees above the horizon), and its **azimuth** (measured in degrees from north 0°, through east 90°,

south 180° and west 270°). Experienced amateurs and professional astronomers also use another system of specifying locations on the celestial sphere, but that need not concern us here, where the simpler method will suffice.

The celestial sphere appears to rotate about an invisible axis, running between the North and South Celestial Poles. The location (i.e., the altitude) of the Celestial Poles depends entirely on the observer's position on Earth or, more specifically, their latitude. The charts in this book are produced for the latitude of 50°N, so the North Celestial Pole (NCP) is 50° above the northern horizon. The fact that the NCP is fixed relative to the horizon means that all the stars within 50° of the pole are always above the horizon and may, therefore, always be seen at night, regardless of the time of year. This northern circumpolar region is an ideal place to begin learning the sky, and ways to identify the circumpolar stars and constellations will be described shortly.

The ecliptic and the zodiac

Another important line on the celestial sphere is the Sun's apparent path against the background stars – in reality the result of the Earth's orbit around the Sun. This is known as the **ecliptic**. The point where the Sun, apparently moving along the ecliptic, crosses the celestial equator from south to north is

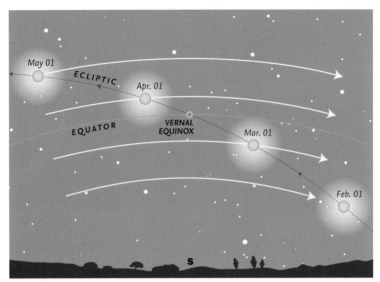

The Sun crossing the celestial equator in spring.

known as the vernal (or spring) equinox, which occurs on March 20. At this time (and at the autumnal equinox, on September 22 or 23, when the Sun crosses the celestial equator from north to south) day and night are almost exactly equal in length. (There is a slight difference, but that need not concern us here.) The vernal equinox is currently located in the constellation of Pisces, and is important in astronomy because it defines the zero point for a system of celestial coordinates, which is, however, not used in this Guide.

The Moon and planets are to be found in a band of sky that extends 8° on either side of the ecliptic. This is because the orbits of the Moon and planets are inclined at various angles to the ecliptic (i.e., to the plane of the Earth's orbit). This band of sky is known as the zodiac and, when originally devised, consisted of twelve **constellations**, all of which were considered to be exactly 30° wide. When the constellation boundaries were formally established by the International Astronomical Union in 1930, the exact extent of most constellations was altered and, nowadays, the ecliptic passes through thirteen constellations.

Because of the boundary changes, the Moon and planets may actually pass through several other constellations that are adjacent to the original twelve.

The constellations

Since ancient times, the celestial sphere has been divided into various constellations, most dating back to antiquity and usually associated with certain myths or legendary people and animals. Nowadays, the boundaries of the constellations have been fixed by international agreement and their names (in Latin) are largely derived from Greek or Roman originals. Some of the names of the most prominent stars are of Greek or Roman origin, but many are derived from Arabic names. Many bright stars have no individual names and, for many years, stars were identified by terms such as 'the star in Hercules' right foot'. A more sensible scheme was introduced by the German astronomer Johannes Bayer in the early seventeenth century. Following his scheme – which is still used today – most of the brightest stars are identified by a Greek letter followed by the genitive form of the

6

constellation's Latin name. An example is the Pole Star, also known as Polaris and α Ursae Minoris (abbreviated α UMi). The Greek alphabet is shown on page 109 with a list of all the constellations that may be seen from latitude 50°N, together with abbreviations, their genitive forms and English names. Other naming schemes exist for fainter stars, but are not used in this book.

Asterisms

Apart from the constellations (88 of which cover the whole sky), certain groups of stars, which may form a part of a larger constellation or cross several constellations, are readily recognizable and have been given individual names. These groups are known as *asterisms*, and the most famous (and well-known) is the 'Plough', the common name for the seven brightest stars in the constellation of Ursa Major, the Great Bear. The names and details of some asterisms mentioned in this book are given in the list on page 110.

Magnitudes

The brightness of a star, planet or other body is frequently given in magnitudes (mag.). This is a mathematically defined scale where larger numbers indicate a fainter object. The scale extends beyond the zero point to negative numbers for very bright objects. (Sirius, the brightest star in the sky is mag. -1.4.) Most observers are able to see stars to about mag. 6, under very clear skies.

The Moon

Although the daily rotation of the Earth carries the sky from east to west, the Moon gradually moves eastwards by approximately its diameter (about half a degree) in an hour. Normally, in its orbit around the Earth, the Moon passes above or below the direct line between Earth and Sun (at New Moon) or outside the area obscured by the Earth's shadow (at Full Moon). Occasionally, however, the three bodies are more-or-less perfectly aligned to give an *eclipse*: a solar eclipse at New Moon or a lunar eclipse at Full Moon. Depending on the exact circumstances, a solar eclipse may be merely partial (when the Moon does not cover the whole of the Sun's disk); annular (when the Moon is too far from Earth in its orbit to appear large enough to hide the whole of the Sun); or total. Total and annular eclipses are visible from very restricted areas of the Earth, but partial eclipses are normally visible over a wider area.

Somewhat similarly, at a lunar eclipse, the Moon may pass through the outer zone of the Earth's shadow, the *penumbra* (in a penumbral eclipse, which is not generally perceptible to the naked eye), so that just part of the Moon is within the darkest part of the Earth's shadow, the *umbra* (in a partial eclipse); or completely within the umbra (in a total eclipse). Unlike solar eclipses, lunar eclipses are visible from large areas of the Earth.

Occasionally, as it moves across the sky, the Moon passes between the Earth and individual planets or distant stars, giving rise to an *occultation*. As with solar eclipses, such occultations are visible from restricted areas of the world.

The planets

Because the planets are always moving against the background stars, they are treated in some detail in the monthly pages and information is given when they are close to other planets, the Moon or any of five bright stars that lie near the ecliptic. Such events are known as *appulses* or, more frequently, as *conjunctions*. (There are technical differences in the way these terms are defined – and should be used – in astronomy, but these need not concern us here.) The positions of the planets are shown for every month on a special chart of the ecliptic.

The term conjunction is also used when a planet is either directly behind or in front of the Sun, as seen from Earth. (Under normal circumstances it will then be invisible.) The conditions of most favourable visibility depend on whether the planet is one of the two known as *inferior planets* (Mercury and Venus) or one of the three *superior planets* (Mars, Jupiter and

Inferior planet.

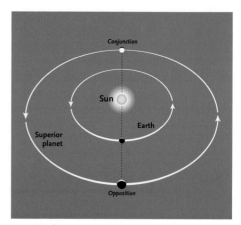

Superior planet.

Saturn) that are covered in detail. (Some details of the fainter superior planets, Uranus and Neptune, are included in this Guide, and special charts are given on page 25.)

The inferior planets are most readily seen at eastern or western **elongation**, when their angular distance from the Sun is greatest. For superior planets, they are best seen at **opposition**, when they are directly opposite the Sun in the sky, and cross the meridian at local midnight.

It is often useful to be able to estimate angles on the sky, and approximate values may be obtained by holding one hand at arm's length. The various angles are shown in the diagram, together with the separations of the various stars in the Plough.

Meteors

At some time or other, nearly everyone has seen a **meteor** – a 'shooting star' – as it flashed across the sky. The particles that cause meteors – known technically as 'meteoroids' – range in size from that of a grain of sand (or even smaller) to the size of a pea. On any night of the year there are occasional meteors, known as **sporadics**, that may travel in any direction. These occur at a rate that is normally between three and eight in an hour. Far more important, however, are **meteor showers**, which occur at fixed periods of the year, when the

Earth encounters a trail of particles left behind by a comet or, very occasionally, by a minor planet (asteroid). Meteors always appear to diverge from a single point on the sky, known as the **radiant**, and the radiants of major showers are shown on the charts. Meteors that come from a circular area 8° in diameter around the radiant are classed as belonging to the particular shower. All others that do not come from that area are sporadics (or, occasionally from another shower that is active at the same time). A list of the major meteor showers is given on page 31.

Although the positions of the various shower radiants are shown on the charts, looking directly at the radiant is not the most effective way of seeing meteors. They are most likely to be noticed if one is looking about 40–45° away from the radiant position. (This is approximately two hand-spans as shown in the diagram for measuring angles.)

Other objects

Certain other objects may be seen with the naked eye under good conditions. Some were given names in antiquity – Praesepe is one example – but many are known by what are called 'Messier numbers', the numbers in a catalogue of nebulous objects compiled by Charles Messier in the late eighteenth century. Some, such as the Andromeda Galaxy, M31, and the Orion Nebula, M42, may be seen

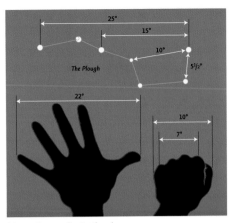

Meteor shower (showing the April Lyrid radiant).

Measuring angles in the sky.

by the naked eye, but all those given in the list will benefit from the use of binoculars. Apart from galaxies, such as M31, which contain thousands of millions of stars, there are also two types of cluster: open clusters, such as M45, the Pleiades, which may consist of a few dozen to some hundreds of stars; and globular clusters, such as M13 in Hercules, which are spherical concentrations of many thousands of stars. One or two gaseous nebulae, consisting of gas illuminated by stars within them, are also visible. The Orion Nebula, M42, is one, and is illuminated by the group of four stars, known as the Trapezium, which may be seen within it by using a good pair of binoculars.

Some interesting objects.

Messier / NGC	Name	Type	Constellation	Maps (months)
—	Hyades	open cluster	Taurus	Sep. – Mar.
—	Double Cluster	open cluster	Perseus	All year
—	Melotte 111 (Coma Cluster)	open cluster	Coma Berenices	Jan. – Aug.
M3	—	globular cluster	Canes Venatici	Jan. – Sep.
M4	—	globular cluster	Scorpius	May – Aug.
M8	Lagoon Nebula	gaseous nebula	Sagittarius	Jun. – Aug.
M11	Wild Duck Cluster	open cluster	Scutum	May – Oct.
M13	Hercules Cluster	globular cluster	Hercules	Feb. – Nov.
M15	—	globular cluster	Pegasus	Jun. – Dec.
M22	—	globular cluster	Sagittarius	Jun. – Sep.
M27	Dumbbell Nebula	planetary nebula	Vulpecula	May – Dec.
M31	Andromeda Galaxy	galaxy	Andromeda	All year
M35	—	open cluster	Gemini	Oct. – May
M42	Orion Nebula	gaseous nebula	Orion	Nov. – Mar.
M44	Praesepe	open cluster	Cancer	Nov. – Jun.
M45	Pleiades	open cluster	Taurus	Aug. – Apr.
M57	Ring Nebula	planetary nebula	Lyra	Apr. – Dec.
M67	—	open cluster	Cancer	Dec. – May
NGC 752	—	open cluster	Andromeda	Jul. – Mar.
NGC 3242	Ghost of Jupiter	planetary nebula	Hydra	Feb. – May

The Northern Circumpolar Constellations

The northern circumpolar stars are the key to starting to identify the constellations. For anyone in the northern hemisphere they are visible at any time of the year, and nearly everyone is familiar with the seven stars of the Plough – known as the Big Dipper in North America – an asterism that forms part of the large constellation of **Ursa Major** (the Great Bear).

Ursa Major

Because of the movement of the stars caused by the passage of the seasons, Ursa Major lies in different parts of the evening sky at different periods of the year. The diagram below shows its position for the four main seasons. The seven stars of the Plough remain visible throughout the year anywhere north of latitude 40°N. Even at the latitude (50°N) for which the charts in this book are drawn, many of the stars in the southern portion of the constellation of Ursa Major are hidden below the horizon for part of the year or (particularly in late summer) cannot be seen late in the night.

Polaris and Ursa Minor

The two stars **Dubhe** and **Merak** (α and β Ursae

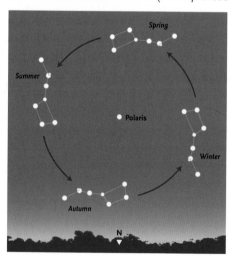

Majoris, respectively), farthest from the 'tail' are known as the 'Pointers'. A line from Merak to Dubhe, extended about five times their separation, leads to the Pole Star, **Polaris**, or α Ursae Minoris. All the stars in the northern sky appear to rotate around it. There are five main stars in the constellation of **Ursa Minor**, and the two farthest from the Pole, **Kochab** and **Pherkad** (β and γ Ursae Minoris, respectively), are known as 'The Guards'.

Cassiopeia

On the opposite of the North Pole from Ursa Major lies **Cassiopeia**. It is highly distinctive, appearing as five stars forming a letter 'W' or 'M' depending on its orientation. Provided the sky is reasonably clear of clouds, you will nearly always be able to see either Ursa Major or Cassiopeia, and thus be able to orientate yourself on the sky.

To find Cassiopeia, start with **Alioth** (ε Ursae Majoris), the first star in the tail of the Great Bear. A line from this star extended through Polaris points directly towards γ Cassiopeiae, the central star of the five.

Cepheus

Although the constellation of **Cepheus** is fully circumpolar, it is not nearly as well-known as Ursa Major, Ursa Minor or Cassiopeia, partly because its stars are fainter. Its shape is rather like the gable end of a house. The line from the Pointers through Polaris, if extended, leads to **Errai** (γ Cephei) at the 'top' of the 'gable'. The brightest star, **Alderamin** (α Cephei) lies in the Milky Way region, at the 'bottom right-hand corner' of the figure.

Draco

The constellation of **Draco** consists of a quadrilateral of stars, known as the 'Head of Draco' (and also the 'Lozenge'), and a long chain of stars forming the neck and body of the dragon. To find the Head of Draco, locate the two stars **Phecda** and **Megrez** (γ and δ Ursae Majoris) in the Plough, opposite the Pointers.

The stars and constellations inside the circle are always above the horizon, seen from our latitude.

Extend a line from Phecda through Megrez by about eight times their separation, right across the sky below the Guards in Ursa Minor, ending at **Grumium** (ξ Draconis) at one corner of the quadrilateral. The brightest star, **Eltanin** (γ Draconis) lies farther to the south. From the head of Draco, the constellation first runs northeast to **Altais** (δ Draconis) and ε Draconis, then doubles back southwards before winding its way through **Thuban** (α Draconis) before ending at **Giausar** (λ Draconis) between the Pointers and Polaris.

The Winter Constellations

The winter sky is dominated by several bright stars and distinctive constellations. The most conspicuous constellation is **Orion**, the main body of which has an hour-glass shape. It straddles the celestial equator and is thus visible from anywhere in the world. The three stars that form the 'Belt' of Orion point down towards the southeast and to **Sirius** (α Canis Majoris), the brightest star in the sky. **Mintaka** (δ Orionis), the star at the northeastern end of the Belt, farthest from Sirius, actually lies just slightly south of the celestial equator.

A line from **Bellatrix** (γ Orionis) at the 'top right-hand corner' of Orion, through **Aldebaran** (α Tauri), past the 'V' of the Hyades cluster, points to the distinctive cluster of bright blue stars known as the **Pleiades**, or the 'Seven Sisters'. Aldebaran is one of the five bright stars that may sometimes be occulted (hidden) by the Moon. Another line from Bellatrix, through

Betelgeuse (α Orionis), if carried right across the sky, points to the constellation of **Leo**, a prominent constellation in the spring sky.

Six bright stars in six different constellations: **Capella** (α Aurigae), **Aldebaran** (α Tauri), **Rigel** (β Orionis), **Sirius** (α Canis Majoris), **Procyon** (Canis Minoris) and **Pollux** (β Gemini) form what is sometimes known as the 'Winter Hexagon'. Pollux is accompanied to the northwest by the slightly fainter star of **Castor** (α Gemini), the second 'Twin'.

In a counterpart to the famous 'Summer Triangle', an almost perfect equilateral triangle, the 'Winter Triangle', is formed by Betelgeuse (α Orionis), Sirius (α Canis Majoris) and Procyon (α Canis Minoris).

Several of the stars in this region of the sky show distinctive tints: Betelgeuse (α Orionis) is reddish, Aldebaran (α Tauri) is orange and Rigel (β Orionis) is blue-white.

The Spring Constellations

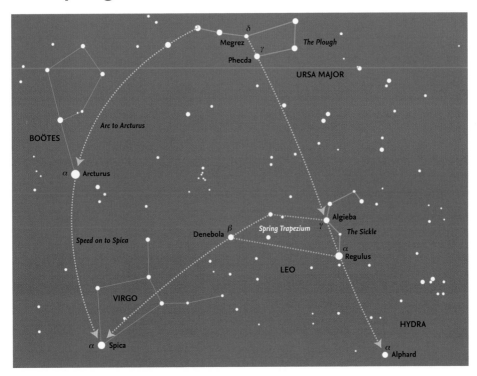

The most prominent constellation in the spring sky is the zodiacal constellation of **Leo**, and its brightest star, **Regulus** (α Leonis), which may be found by extending a line from Megrez and Phecda (δ and γ Ursae Majoris, respectively) – the two stars on the opposite side of the bowl of the Plough from the Pointers – down to the southeast. Regulus forms the 'dot' of the 'backward question mark' known as 'the Sickle'. Regulus, like Aldebaran in Taurus is one of the bright stars that lie close to the ecliptic, and that are occasionally occulted by the Moon. The same line from Ursa Major to Regulus, if continued, leads to **Alphard** (α Hydrae), the brightest star in **Hydra**, the largest of the 88 constellations.

The shape formed by the body of Leo is sometimes known as the 'Spring Trapezium'. At the other end of the constellation from Regulus is **Denebola** (β Leonis), and the line forming the back of the constellation through Denebola points to the bright star **Spica** (α Virginis) in the constellation of **Virgo**. A saying that helps to locate Spica is well-known to astronomers: 'Arc to Arcturus and then speed on to Spica.' This suggests following the arc of the tail of Ursa Major to Arcturus and then on to Spica. **Arcturus** (α Boötis) is actually the brightest star in the northern hemisphere of the sky. (Although other stars, such as Sirius, are brighter, they are all in the southern hemisphere.) Overall, the constellation of **Boötes** is sometimes described as 'kite-shaped' or 'shaped like the letter P'.

Although Spica is the brightest star in the zodiacal constellation of Virgo, the rest of the constellation is not particularly distinct, consisting of a rough quadrilateral of moderately bright stars and some fainter lines of stars extending outwards.

The Summer Constellations

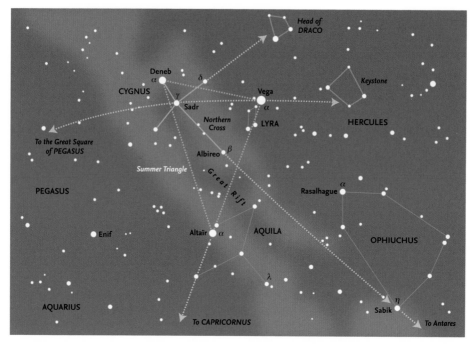

On summer nights, the three bright stars **Deneb** (α Cygni), **Vega** (α Lyrae) and **Altair** (α Aquilae) form the striking 'Summer Triangle'. The constellations of **Cygnus** (the Swan) and **Aquila** (the Eagle) represent birds 'flying' down the length of the Milky Way. This part of the Milky Way contains the **Great Rift**, an elongated dark region, where the light from distant stars is obscured by intervening dust. The dark Rift is clearly visible even to the naked eye.

The most prominent stars of Cygnus are sometimes known as the 'Northern Cross' (as a counterpart to the 'Southern Cross' – the constellation of Crux – in the southern hemisphere). The central line of Cygnus through **Albireo** (β Cygni), extended well to the southwest, points to **Sabik** (η Ophiuchi) in the large, sprawling constellation of Ophiuchus (the Serpent Bearer) and beyond to **Antares** (α Scorpii) in the constellation of **Scorpius**. Like Cepheus, the shape of Ophiuchus somewhat resembles the gable-end of a house, and the

brightest star **Rasalhague** (α Ophiuchi) is at the 'apex' of the 'gable'.

A line from the central star of Cygnus, **Sadr** (γ Cygni) through δ Cygni, in the northwestern 'wing' points towards the Head of Draco, and is another way of locating that part of the constellation. Another line from Sadr to Vega indicates the central portion, 'The Keystone', of the constellation of **Hercules**. An arc through the same stars, in the opposite direction, points towards the constellation of **Pegasus**, and more specifically to the 'Great Square of Pegasus'.

Aquila is less conspicuous than Cygnus and consists of a diamond shape of stars, representing the body and wings of the eagle, together with a rather faint star, λ Aquilae, marking the 'head'. **Lyra** (the Lyre) mainly consists of Vega (α Lyrae) and a small quadrilateral of stars to its southeast. Continuation of a line from Vega through Altair indicates the zodiacal constellation of **Capricornus**.

The Autumn Constellations

During the autumn season, the most striking feature is the 'Great Square of Pegasus', an almost perfect rectangle on the sky, forming the main body of the constellation of **Pegasus**. However, the star at the northeastern corner, **Alpheratz**, is actually α Andromedae, and part of the adjacent constellation of **Andromeda**. A line from **Scheat** (β Pegasi) at the northeastern corner of the Square, through **Matar** (η Pegasi), points in the general direction of Cygnus. A crooked line of stars leads from **Markab** (α Pegasi) through **Homam** (ζ Pegasi) and **Biham** (θ Pegasi) to **Enif** (ε Pegasi). A line from Markab through the last star in the Square, **Algenib** (γ Pegasi) points in the general direction of the five stars, including **Menkar** (α Ceti) that form the 'tail' of the constellation of **Cetus** (the Whale). A ring of seven stars lying below the southern side of the Great Square is known as 'the Circlet', part of the constellation of **Pisces** (the Fishes).

Extending the line of the western side of the Great Square towards the south leads to the isolated bright star, **Fomalhaut** (α Piscis Austrini), in the Southern Fish. Following the line of the eastern side of the Great Square towards the north leads to Cassiopeia while, in the other direction, it points towards **Diphda** (β Ceti), which is actually the brightest star in Cetus.

Three bright stars leading northeast from Alpheratz form the main body of the constellation of **Andromeda**. Continuation of that line leads towards the constellation of **Perseus** and **Mirfak** (α Persei). Running southwards from Mirfak is a chain of stars, one of which is the famous variable star **Algol** (β Persei). Farther east, an arc of stars leads to the prominent cluster of the **Pleiades**, in the constellation of **Taurus**.

Between Andromeda and Cetus lie the two small constellations of **Triangulum** (the Triangle) and **Aries** (the Ram).

The Moon at First Quarter.

The Moon

The monthly pages include diagrams showing the phase of the Moon for every day of the month, and also indicate the day in the **lunation** (or *age* of the Moon), which begins at New Moon. Although the main features of the surface – the light highlands and the dark maria (seas) – may be seen with the naked eye, far more features may be detected with the use of binoculars or any telescope. The many craters are best seen when they are close to the **terminator** (the boundary between the illuminated and the non-illuminated areas of the surface), when the Sun rises or sets over any particular region of the Moon and the crater walls or central peaks cast strong shadows. Most features become difficult to see at Full Moon, although this is the best time to see the bright ray systems surrounding certain craters. Accompanying the Moon map on the following pages is a list of prominent features, including the days in the lunation when features are normally close to the terminator and thus easiest to see. A few bright features

such as Linné and Proclus, visible when well illuminated, are also listed. One feature, Rupes Recta (the Straight Wall) is readily visible only when it casts a shadow with light from the east, appearing as a light line when illuminated from the opposite direction.

The dates of visibility vary slightly through the effects of **libration**. Because the Moon's orbit is inclined to the Earth's equator and also because it moves in an ellipse, the Moon appears to rock slightly from side to side (and nod up and down). Features near the **limb** (the edge of the Moon) may vary considerably in their location and visibility. (This is easily noticeable with Mare Crisium and the craters Tycho and Plato.) Another effect is that at crescent phases before and after New Moon, the normally non-illuminated portion of the Moon receives a certain amount of light, reflected from the Earth. This **Earthshine** may enable certain bright features (such as Aristarchus, Kepler and Copernicus) to be detected even though they are not illuminated by sunlight.

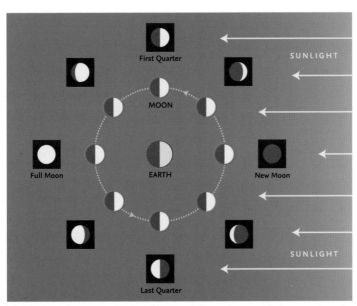

The Moon phases. *During its orbit around the Earth we see different portions of the illuminated side of the Moon's surface.*

Map of the Moon

The numbers indicate the age of the Moon when features are usually best visible.

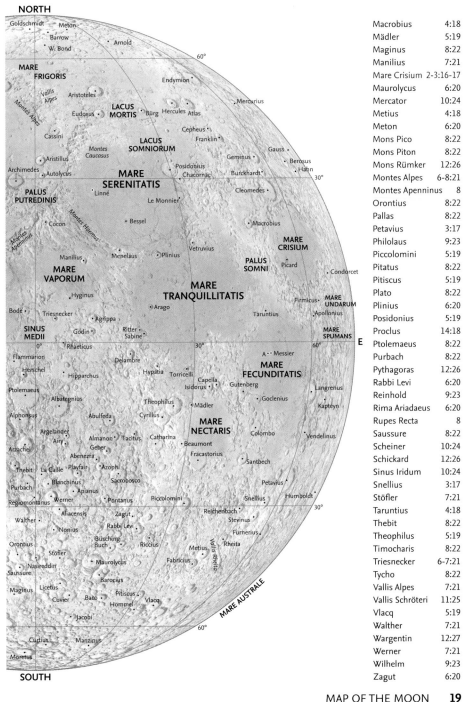

Eclipses in 2021

Lunar eclipses

There are two lunar eclipses in 2021, one total and one that is technically partial, although most of the Moon will pass within the **umbra** and appear dark. These eclipses are shown in the diagrams opposite. In both cases, mid-eclipse occurs over the middle of the Pacific Ocean. The first (on May 26) will be visible from the central and southern Pacific, and the second (on November 19) from the northern region. During that partial eclipse, a small portion will remain within the **penumbra**.

Solar eclipses

There are two solar eclipses in 2021, the central lines being visible only from the Earth's polar regions. The **annular** solar eclipse of June 10 occurs over Arctic Canada (with maximum eclipse at 10:43 UT over northwest Greenland), continuing over the Arctic Ocean and ending over Siberia. The partial phases will be visible over the northern Atlantic, northern Europe and the last stages after sunrise in parts of the northeastern United States and Canada.

The second eclipse on December 4 is in the far south. It begins and ends over the Southern Ocean and crosses West Antarctica. Maximum eclipse occurs (at 07:33 UT) over the coast of the Weddell Sea. The partial phases are visible over a large region of the Southern Ocean and East Antarctica.

A lunar eclipse occurs when the Moon passes through the Earth's shadow (top). When it passes between the Earth and the Sun (bottom) there is a solar eclipse.

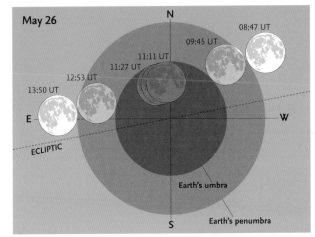

A total lunar eclipse occurs on May 26, not visible from Great Britain. Generally visible from the Pacific, just the beginning is visible from the West Coast of North America. Most of the eclipse is seen from Australia and New Zealand, including mid-eclipse (at 11:18 UT). The very end becomes visible from Indonesia and eastern Asia.

The lunar eclipse on November 19 is partial, because a very small portion of the Moon remains outside the umbra, in the penumbra. This eclipse will be visible from North America; at mid eclipse (09:03 UT) the Moon will be low for observers on the East Coast. Only the extreme West Coast (and eastern Asia, together with northern Australia) will see the final phases.

A sequence of five images of the Moon, taken by Akira Fuji, showing the progression of the Moon (from right to left: west to east) through the Earth's shadow.

The Planets in 2021

Mercury and Venus

Although **Venus** may be prominent in the sky for many months at a time, the innermost planet, **Mercury**, is readily visible only at certain elongations. Not every one is favourable. In 2021, for example, Mercury comes to greatest elongation seven times, but it is most visible at four of those only. These occasions are shown on the diagrams below.

Venus is prominent throughout 2021, but has a single greatest elongation on October 29, not very favourable from the UK, and shown in the last diagram on this page.

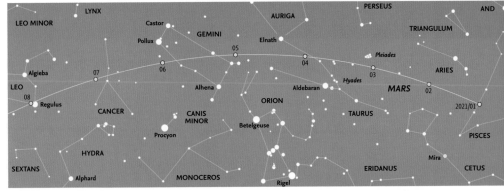

The path of Mars from January to August 2021. Later in the year, Mars is too close to the Sun to observe.

Mars

Because its orbit lies outside that of the Earth, so it takes longer to complete a full orbit, **Mars** does not come to opposition every year, as is the case in 2021. Instead, it remains in the sky for many months at a time, moving slowly along the ecliptic. The planet's path in 2021 is shown on the large chart given here. It begins the year at magnitude -0.2, but then fades to mag. 1.8 in August, when it becomes too close to the Sun to be visible.

Oppositions occur during a period of *retrograde motion*, when the planet appears to move westwards against the pattern of distant stars. As mentioned, there is no opposition

in 2021, and the planet reverted to **direct motion** (eastward) on 17 November 2020.

Because of its eccentric orbit, which carries it at very differing distances from the Sun (and Earth), not all oppositions of Mars are equally favourable for observation. The relative positions of Mars and the Earth are shown here. It will be seen that the opposition of 2018 was very close and thus favourable for observation, and that of 2020 was also reasonably good. By comparison, opposition in 2027 will be at a far greater distance, so the planet will appear much smaller.

Between June 22 and June 25, Mars crosses the open star cluster M44 (Praesepe) in Cancer. All stars brighter than magnitude 8.5 are shown.

The oppositions of Mars between 2018 and 2033. As the illustration shows, there is no opposition in 2021.

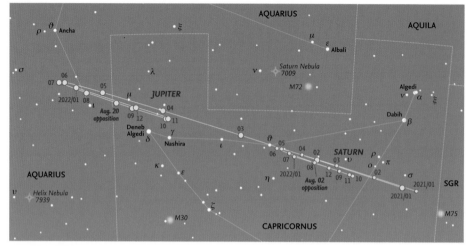

The paths of Jupiter and Saturn in 2021. Background stars are shown down to magnitude 6.5.

Jupiter and Saturn

In 2021, **Jupiter** and **Saturn** are in the same region of sky. Jupiter moves right across **Capricornus** and into **Aquarius**, where it begins to retrograde on June 21. It comes to opposition, just within Aquarius, on August 20, and resumes direct motion on October 30. Saturn, by contrast, remains within Capricornus, retrograding from May 24 to October 19, with opposition on August 2.

Jupiter's four large satellites are readily visible in binoculars. Not all four are visible all the time, sometimes hidden behind the planet or invisible in front of it. **Io**, the closest to Jupiter, orbits in just under 1.8 days, and **Callisto**, the farthest away, takes about 16.7 days. In between are **Europa** (*c.* 3.6 days) and **Ganymede**, the largest, (*c.* 7.1 days). The diagram shows the satellites' motions around the time of opposition.

Jupiter and the four Galilean satellites, photographed by Jan Sandberg with a 10-inch (254-mm) Schmidt-Cassegrain telescope.

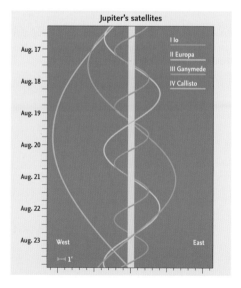

Uranus and Neptune

Uranus begins the year (at mag. 5.7) retrograding in **Aries**, in which constellation it remains for the whole year. It starts direct motion on January 16 and does not begin retrograding until August 20. It reaches opposition (mag. 5.6) on November 4 (at New Moon). It is still retrograding at the end of the year, when it is again mag. 5.7.

Neptune is in **Aquarius** throughout 2021, beginning at mag. 7.9. It moves eastwards until June 27, when it begins to retrograde. It comes to opposition (at mag. 7.8) on September 14 (just after First Quarter, so moonlight should not interfere greatly). It resumes direct motion on December 4, and is mag. 7.9 at the end of the year.

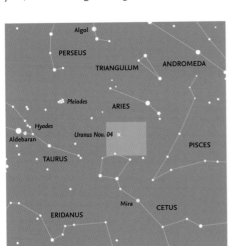

In 2021, Uranus may be found in the southern part of the constellation of Aries.

The path of Uranus in 2021. Uranus comes to opposition on November 4. All stars brighter than magnitude 7.5 are shown.

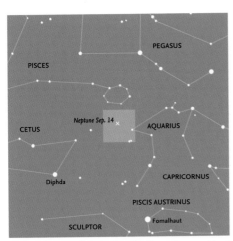

In 2021, Neptune is to be found in the easternmost part of the constellation of Aquarius.

The path of Neptune in 2021. Neptune comes to opposition on September 14. All stars brighter than magnitude 8.5 are shown.

Minor Planets in 2021

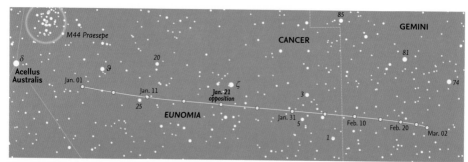

The path of the minor planet (15) Eunomia around its opposition on January 21 (mag. 8.5). Background stars are shown down to magnitude 9.5.

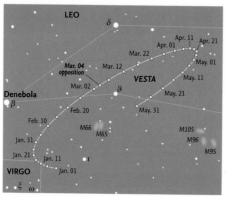

The path of the minor planet (4) Vesta around its opposition on March 4 (mag. 6.0). Background stars are shown down to magnitude 7.5.

In 2021, five minor planets become bright enough to be visible at opposition. These (in date order of opposition) are: *(15) Eunomia* in *Cancer* on January 21; *(4) Vesta* in *Leo* on March 4; *(6) Hebe* in *Aquila* on July 17; *(2) Pallas* in *Pisces* on September 11; and *(1) Ceres*, the dwarf planet on November 27 in *Taurus*. The locations are shown on the small charts at the bottom of page 27. During the oppositions of Eunomia, Vesta and Hebe there will be some interference from moonlight and these minor planets will then be easier to detect some time before or after the opposition.

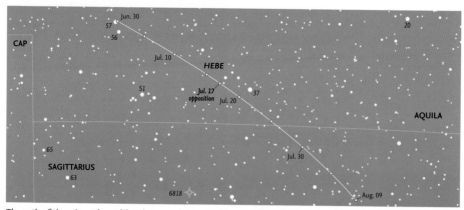

The path of the minor planet (6) Hebe around its opposition on July 17 (mag. 8.4). Background stars are shown down to magnitude 9.5.

The path of the minor planet (2) Pallas around its opposition on September 11 (mag. 8.5). Background stars are shown down to magnitude 9.5. →

The path of the dwarf planet (1) Ceres around its opposition on November 27 (mag. 7.0). Background stars are shown down to magnitude 8.5.

↓

The five small charts show the areas covered by the larger maps on these pages, in a lighter blue. The white cross shows the position of the minor planet at the day of its opposition.

Comets in 2021

Although comets may occasionally become very striking objects in the sky, their occurrence and particularly the existence or length of any tail and their overall magnitude are notoriously difficult to predict. Naturally, it is only possible to predict the return of periodic comets (whose names have the prefix 'P'). Many comets appear unexpectedly (these have names with the prefix 'C'). Bright, readily visible comets such as C/1995 Y1 Hyakutake, C/1995 01 Hale-Bopp or C/2006 P1 McNaught

(sometimes known as the Great Comet of 2007) are rare. Comet C/2006 P1 McNaught was notable for its multiple tail structure. Most periodic comets are faint and only a very small number ever become bright enough to be readily visible with the naked eye or with binoculars.

The comet most likely to become visible in 2021 is **67P/Churyumov-Gerasimenko**. This is the comet visited and investigated by ESA's Rosetta space probe in 2014–2016.

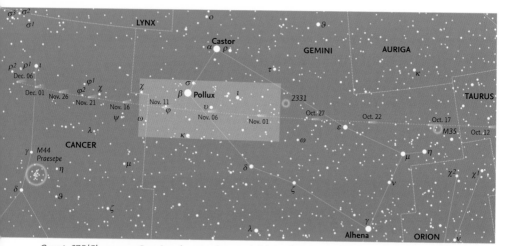

Comet 67P/Churyumov-Gerasimenko may become brighter than its predicted mag. 9.9, around November 6. Its path is shown here from October 12 to December 6. Background stars are shown down to magnitude 8.0. The area covered by the more detailed map below is shown in a lighter blue. On that map, all stars down to magnitude 10.5 are shown.

Comet 67P/Churyumov-Gerasimenko, photographed by Damian Peach on 21 November 2015, while in the constellation of Leo, approximately one degree east of iota (ι) Leonis.

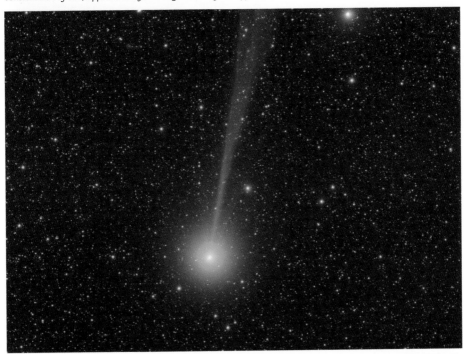

Comet C/2014 Q2 Lovejoy, which reached naked-eye visibility, photographed on 20 December 2014, when in Columba, by Damian Peach.

Introduction to the Month-by-Month Guide

The monthly charts

The pages devoted to each month contain a pair of charts showing the appearance of the night sky, looking north and looking south. The charts (as with all the charts in this book) are drawn for the latitude of 50°N, so observers farther north will see slightly more of the sky on the northern horizon, and slightly less on the southern. These areas are, of course, those most likely to be affected by poor observing conditions caused by haze, mist or smoke. In addition, stars close to the horizon are always dimmed by atmospheric absorption, so sometimes the faintest stars marked on the charts may not be visible.

The three times shown for each chart require a little explanation. The charts are drawn to show the appearance at 23:00 GMT for the 1st of each month. The same appearance will apply an hour earlier (22:00 GMT) on the 15th, and yet another hour earlier (21:00 GMT) at the end of the month (shown as the 1st of the following month). GMT is identical to the Universal Time (UT) used by astronomers around the world. In Europe, Summer Time is introduced in March, so the March charts apply to 23:00 GMT on March 1, 22:00 GMT on March 15, but 22:00 BST (British Summer Time) on April 1. The change back from Summer Time (in Europe) occurs in October, so the charts for that month apply to 00:00 BST for October 1, 23:00 BST for October 15, and 21:00 GMT for November 1.

The charts may be used for earlier or later times during the night. To observe two hours earlier, use the charts for the preceding month; for two hours later, the charts for the next month.

Meteors

Details of specific meteor showers are given in the months when they come to maximum, regardless of whether they begin or end in other months. Note that not all the respective radiants are marked on the charts for that

particular month, because the radiants may be below the horizon, or lie in constellations that are not readily visible during the month of maximum. For this reason, special charts for the Eta (η) and Delta (δ) Aquariids (May and July, respectively) and the Leonids (November) are given here. As explained earlier, however, meteors from such showers may still be seen, because the most effective region for seeing meteors is some 40–45° away from the radiant, and that area of sky may well be above the horizon. A table of the best meteor showers visible during the year is also given here. The rates given are based on the properties of the meteor streams, and are those that an experienced observer might see under ideal conditions. Generally, the observed rates will be far less.

Shower	Dates of activity 2021	Date of maximum 2021	Possible hourly rate
Quadrantids	December 28 to January 12	January 3–4	120
April Lyrids	April 13–29	April 22	18
η-Aquariids	April 18 to May 27	May 6	40
α-Capricornids	July 2 to August 14	July 30	5
Southern δ-Aquariids	July 13 to August 24	July 30	< 25
Perseids	July 16 to August 23	August 12–13	150
α-Aurigids	August 28 to September 5	September 1	6
Southern Taurids	September 10 to November 20	October 10	< 5
Orionids	October 1 to November 6	October 21	25
Draconids	October 7–11	October 8–9	var.
Northern Taurids	October 20 to December 10	November 12	< 5
Leonids	November 5–29	November 17–18	< 15
Geminids	December 3–16	December 14	120+
Ursids	December 17–26	December 22–23	< 10

Meteors that are brighter than magnitude -4 (approximately the maximum magnitude reached by Venus) are known as *fireballs* or *bolides*. Examples are shown on pages 32, 35 and 77. Fireballs sometimes cause sonic booms that may be heard some time after the meteor is seen.

The photographs

As an aid to identification – especially as some people find it difficult to relate charts to the actual stars they see in the sky – one or more photographs of constellations visible in certain specific months are included. It should be noted, however, that because of the limitations of the photographic and printing processes, and the differences between the sensitivity of different individuals to faint starlight (especially in their ability to detect different colours), and the degree to which they have become adapted to the dark, the apparent brightness of stars in the photographs will not necessarily precisely match that seen by any one observer.

The Moon calendar

The Moon calendar is largely self-explanatory. It shows the phase of the Moon for every day of the month, with the exact times (in Universal Time) of New Moon, First Quarter, Full Moon and Last Quarter. Because the times are calculated from the Moon's actual orbital parameters, some of the times shown

will, naturally, fall during daylight, but any difference is too small to affect the appearance of the Moon on that date. Also shown is the *age* of the Moon (the day in the *lunation*), beginning at New Moon, which may be used to determine the best time for observation of specific lunar features.

The Moon

The section on the Moon includes details of any lunar or solar eclipses that may occur during the month (visible from anywhere on Earth). Similar information is given about any important occultations. Mainly, however, this section summarizes when the Moon passes close to planets or the five prominent stars close to the ecliptic. The dates when the Moon is closest to the Earth (at *perigee*) and farthest from it (at *apogee*) are shown in the monthly calendars, and only mentioned here when they are particularly significant, such as the nearest and farthest during the year.

The planets and minor planets

Brief details are given of the location, movement and brightness of the planets from Mercury to Saturn throughout the month. None of the planets can, of course, be seen when they are close to the Sun, so such periods are generally noted. All of the planets may sometimes lie on the opposite side of the Sun to the Earth (at superior conjunction), but

A fireball (with flares approximately as bright as the Full Moon), photographed against a weak auroral display by D. Buczynski from Tarbat Ness in Scotland on 22 January 2017.

in the case of the inferior planets, Mercury and Venus, they may also pass between the Earth and the Sun (at inferior conjunction) and are invisible for a period of time, the length of which varies from conjunction to conjunction. Those two planets are normally easiest to see around either eastern or western elongation, in the evening or morning sky, respectively. Not every elongation is favourable, so although every elongation is listed, only those where observing conditions are favourable are shown in the individual diagrams of events.

The dates at which the superior planets reverse their motion (from direct motion to **retrograde**, and retrograde to direct) and of opposition (when a planet generally reaches its maximum brightness) are given. Some planets, especially distant Saturn, may spend most or all of the year in a single constellation. Jupiter and Saturn are normally easiest to see around opposition, which occurs every year. Mars, by contrast, moves relatively rapidly against the background stars and in some years never comes to opposition.

Uranus is normally magnitude 5.7–5.9, and thus at the limit of naked-eye visibility under exceptionally dark skies, but bright enough to be readily visible in binoculars. Because its orbital period is so long (over 84 years), Uranus moves only slowly along the ecliptic, and often remains within a single constellation for a whole year. The chart on page 25 shows its position during 2021.

Similar considerations apply to Neptune, although it is always fainter (generally magnitude 7.8–8.0), still visible in most binoculars. It takes about 164.8 years to complete one orbit of the Sun. As with Uranus, it frequently spends a complete year in one constellation. Its chart is also on page 25.

In any year, few minor planets ever become bright enough to be detectable in binoculars. Just one, (4) Vesta, on rare occasions brightens sufficiently for it to be visible to the naked eye. Our limit for visibility is magnitude 9.0 and details and charts are given for those objects that exceed that magnitude during the year, normally around opposition. To assist in recognition of a planet or minor planet as it moves against the background stars, the latter are shown to a fainter magnitude than the object at opposition. Minor-planet charts for 2021 are on pages 26 and 27.

The ecliptic charts

Although the ecliptic charts are primarily designed to show the positions and motions of the major planets, they also show the motion of the Sun during the month. The light-tinted area shows the area of the sky that is invisible during daylight, but the darker area gives an indication of which constellations are likely to be visible at some time of the night. The closer a planet is to the border between dark and light, the more difficult it will be to see in the twilight.

The monthly calendar

For each month, a calendar shows details of significant events, including when planets are close to one another in the sky, close to the Moon, or close to any one of five bright stars that are spaced along the ecliptic. The times shown are given in Universal Time (UT), always used by astronomers throughout the year, and which is identical to Greenwich Mean Time (GMT). So during the summer months, they do not show Summer Time, which will always be one hour later than the time shown.

The diagrams of interesting events

Each month, a number of diagrams show the appearance of the sky when certain events take place. However, the exact positions of celestial objects and their separations greatly depend on the observer's position on Earth. When the Moon is one of the objects involved, because it is relatively close to Earth, there may be very significant changes from one location to another. Close approaches between planets or between a planet and a star are less affected by changes of location, which may thus be ignored.

The diagrams showing the appearance of the sky are drawn for the latitude of London, so will be approximately correct for most of Britain and Europe. However, for an observer farther north (say, Edinburgh), a planet or star listed as being north of the Moon will appear even farther north, whereas one south of the Moon will appear closer to it – or may even be hidden (occulted) by it. For an observer farther south than London, there will be corresponding changes in the opposite direction: for a star or planet south of the Moon, the separation will increase, and for one north of the Moon, the separation will decrease. This is particularly important when occultations occur, which may be visible from one location, but not another. However, there are no major occultations visible from Britain in 2021.

Ideally, details should be calculated for each individual observer, but this is obviously impractical. In fact, positions and separations are actually calculated for a theoretical observer located at the centre of the Earth.

So the details given regarding the positions of the various bodies should be used as a guide to their location. A similar situation arises with the times that are shown. These are calculated according to certain technical criteria, which need not concern us here. However, they do not necessarily indicate the exact time when two bodies are closest together. Similarly, dates and times are given, even if they fall in daylight, when the objects are likely to be completely invisible. However, such times do give an indication that the objects concerned will be in the same general area of the sky during both the preceding and the following nights.

Data used in this Guide

The data given in this Guide, such as timings and distances between objects, have been computed with a program developed by the US Naval Observatory in Washington D.C., widely regarded as the most accurate computation. As such, the data may differ slightly from information given elsewhere.

Key to the symbols used on the monthy star maps.

January 01   23:00 GMT
January 15   22:00 GMT
February 01   21:00 GMT

January – Looking North

January – Looking North

Most of the important circumpolar constellations are easy to see in the northern sky at this time of year. **Ursa Major** stands more-or-less vertically above the horizon in the northeast, with the zodiacal constellation of **Leo** rising in the east. To the north, the stars of **Ursa Minor** lie below **Polaris** (the Pole Star). The head of **Draco** is low on the northern horizon, but may be difficult to see unless observing conditions are good. Both **Cepheus** and **Cassiopeia** are readily visible in the northwest, and even the faint constellation of **Camelopardalis** is high enough in the sky for it to be easily visible.

Near the zenith is the constellation of **Auriga** (the Charioteer), with brilliant **Capella** (α Aurigae), directly overhead. Slightly to the west of Capella lies a small triangle of fainter stars, known as 'The Kids'. (Ancient mythological representations of Auriga show him carrying two young goats.) Together with the northernmost bright star in Taurus, **Elnath** (β Tauri), the body of Auriga forms a large pentagon on the sky, with The Kids lying on the western side. Farther down towards the west are the constellations of **Perseus** and **Andromeda**, and the Great Square of Pegasus is approaching the horizon.

Meteors

The Quadrantids: One of the strongest and most consistent meteor showers of the year occurs in January, visible December 28 to January 12, with maximum on January 3–4. They are brilliant, bluish and yellowish-white and at maximum may even reach a rate of 120 meteors per hour. At maximum on January 3–4 the Moon is waning gibbous, a few days before Last Quarter, so there will be fairly considerable interference from moonlight. The parent object is minor planet 2003 EH_1.

The shower is named after the former constellation **Quadrans Muralis** (the Mural Quadrant), an early form of astronomical

A late Quadrantid fireball, photographed from Portmahomack, Ross-shire, Scotland on 15 January 2018 at 23:44 UT.

Ursa Major, the key constellation to navigating the northern sky.

instrument. The Quadrantid meteor radiant, marked on the chart, is now within the northernmost part of **Boötes**, roughly half-way between θ Boötis and τ Herculis.

CANES VENATICI

M3

URSA MAJOR

COMA
BERENICES

Melotte 111

LEO MINOR

CAMELOPARDALIS

ZENITH

Capella
The
Kids

CASSIOPEIA

Double Cluster

PERSEUS

Algol

Andromeda Galaxy
M31

ANDROMEDA

Alpheratz

Great Square
of Pegasus

PEGASUS

W

LYNX

AURIGA

Elnath

NGC 752

TRIANGULUM

Hamal

ARIES

PISCES

ECLIPTIC

MARS

Denebola

LEO

Algieba

Regulus

Castor

Pollux

GEMINI

M35

Pleiades

TAURUS

Hyades

Aldebaran

MARS

CETUS

Mira

VIRGO

E

CANCER

M44
Praesepe

M67

Alhena

CANIS
MINOR

Procyon

MONOCEROS

Betelgeuse

ORION

M42
Orion Nebula

Rigel

ERIDANUS

FORNAX

SEXTANS

HYDRA

Alphard

CANIS
MAJOR

Sirius

Adhara

LEPUS

CAELUM

PYXIS

PUPPIS

COLUMBA

S

January 01   23:00 GMT
January 15   22:00 GMT

January – Looking South

The southern sky is dominated by **Orion**, prominent during the winter months, visible at some time during the night. It is highly distinctive, with a line of three stars that form the 'Belt'. To most observers, the bright star **Betelgeuse** (α Orionis), shows a reddish tinge, in contrast to the brilliant bluish-white **Rigel** (β Orionis). The three stars of the belt lie directly south of the celestial equator. A vertical line of three 'stars' forms the 'Sword' that hangs south of the Belt. With good viewing, the central 'star' appears as a hazy spot, even to the naked eye, and is actually the **Orion Nebula**. Binoculars reveal the four stars of the Trapezium, which illuminate the nebula.

Orion's Belt points up to the northwest towards **Taurus** (the Bull) and orange-tinted **Aldebaran** (α Tauri). Close to Aldebaran, there is a conspicuous 'V' of stars, called the **Hyades** cluster. (Despite appearances, Aldebaran is not part of the cluster.) Farther along, the same line from Orion passes below a bright cluster of stars, the **Pleiades**, or Seven Sisters. Even the smallest pair of binoculars reveals this as a beautiful group of bluish-white stars. The two most conspicuous of the other stars in Taurus lie directly above Orion, and form an elongated triangle with Aldebaran. The northernmost, **Elnath** (β Tauri), was once considered to be part of the constellation of **Auriga**.

The constellation of Orion dominates the sky during this period of the year, and is a useful starting point for recognizing other constellations in the southern sky. Here, orange Betelgeuse, blue-white Rigel and the pinkish Orion Nebula are prominent. Orion can be found in the southern part of the sky (see page 36).

The Moon's phases for January

					Last Quarter								**New Moon**		
01	02	03	04	05	06 09:37	07	08	09	10	11	12	13 05:00	14	15	16
Day 18	Day 19	Day 20	Day 21	Day 22	Day 23	Day 24	Day 25	Day 26	Day 27	Day 28	Day 29	Day 1	Day 2	Day 3	Day 4

		First Quarter					**Full Moon**						
17	18	19	20 21:02	21	22	23	24	25	26	27	28 19:16	29	30	31
Day 5	Day 6	Day 7	Day 8	Day 9	Day 10	Day 11	Day 12	Day 13	Day 14	Day 15	Day 16	Day 17	Day 18	Day 19

January – Moon and Planets

The Earth

The Earth reaches perihelion (the closest point to the Sun in its annual orbit) on 2 January 2021, at 13:51 Universal Time. Its distance is then 0.983257 AU (147,093,163 km).

The Moon

On January 2, the waning gibbous Moon passes 4.7° north of **Regulus** in **Leo**. On January 6, at Last Quarter, it is north of **Spica** in **Virgo**. On January 10, just before New Moon, it passes 6.0° north of **Antares**. On January 21 it is 5.1° south of **Mars** and then 3.3° south of **Uranus**. On January 24 (waxing gibbous) it passes 4.8° north of **Aldebaran** in **Taurus**, and then, on January 27 (one day before Full) it is south of **Pollux** in **Gemini**. On January 30, waning gibbous, it is again north of Regulus.

The planets

In the evening sky, **Mercury** reaches greatest eastern elongation at mag. -0.7 on January 24. **Venus** (mag. -3.9), initially in **Ophiuchus**, moves closer to the Sun. **Mars** moves from **Pisces** to **Aries**, fading from mag. -0.2 to 0.4. **Jupiter** (mag. -2.0) is in **Capricornus**, too close to the Sun to be visible. **Saturn**, also in Capricornus, is invisible near the Sun. **Uranus** (mag. 5.7 to 5.8) is initially retrograding in Aries, but resumes direct motion on January 16. **Neptune** (mag. 7.9) is in **Aquarius**, where it remains for the whole year. On January 21, minor planet **(15) Eunomia** is at opposition (mag. 8.5) in **Cancer** (see the chart on page 26).

The path of the Sun and the planets along the ecliptic in January.

01–12		Quadrantid meteor shower
02	13:51	Earth at perihelion (0.983257 AU = 147,093,163 km)
02	22:28	Regulus 4.7°S of Moon
03–04		Quadrantid shower maximum
06	09:37	Last Quarter
06	18:33	Spica 7.0°S of Moon
09	15:37	Moon at perigee (367,387 km)
09	21:00 *	Mercury 1.7°S of Saturn
10	02:38	Antares 6.0°S of Moon
11	11:00 *	Mercury 1.5°S of Jupiter
11	20:09	Venus 1.5°N of Moon
13	05:00	New Moon
13	20:52	Saturn 3.2°N of Moon
14	01:27	Jupiter 3.3°N of Moon
14	08:13	Mercury 2.3°N of Moon
17	06:14	Neptune 4.5°N of Moon
20	21:02	First Quarter
21	05:37	Mars 5.1°N of Moon
21	06:24	Uranus 3.3°N of Moon
21	13:11	Moon at apogee (404,360 km)
21	18:37	Minor planet (15) Eunomia at opposition (mag. 8.5)
22	01:02	Uranus 1.7°S of Mars
24	00:00 *	Mercury at greatest elongation (18.6°E, mag. -0.7)
24	03:01	Saturn in conjunction with the Sun
24	05:13	Aldebaran 4.8°S of Moon
27	16:18	Pollux 3.8°N of Moon
28	19:16	Full Moon
29	01:40	Jupiter in conjunction with the Sun
30	05:25	Regulus 4.6°S of Moon

These objects are close together for an extended

Morning 7:30

January 10 • *Shortly before sunrise, the Moon is between Antares and Sabik (η Oph), Venus (mag. -3.9) is low in the southeast.*

Evening 23:30

January 2 • *The Moon is halfway between Regulus and Algieba. Denebola is a little lower in the east.*

Evening 23:30

Evening 16:50

January 14 • *The narrow crescent Moon with Mercury, Jupiter and*

January 20–21 • *The Moon passes Mars and Uranus (mag. 5.8). Background stars*

Evening 19:00

January 27 • *The Moon lines up with Castor and Pollux, in*

CRATER

ECLIPTIC

LEO

Denebola

Melotte 111

COMA
BERENICES

M3

BOÖTES

Arcturus

VIRGO

E

Regulus

Algieba

LEO MINOR

CANES VENATICI

The Plough

Alphecca

CORONA
BOREALIS

M13

HERCULES

CANCER

URSA
MAJOR

Pollux

Castor

LYNX

ZENITH

DRACO

Vega

GEMINI

CAMELOPARDALIS

URSA
MINOR

Polaris

LYRA

N

M35

Capella

CEPHEUS

CYGNUS

Deneb

Elnath

AURIGA

The Kids

Double Cluster

CASSIOPEIA

Caph

LACERTA

ORION

Algol

PERSEUS

NGC 752

Andromeda Galaxy

M31

ANDROMEDA

Pleiades

Aldebaran

Hyades

Hamal

TRIANGULUM

PEGASUS

Alpheratz

MARS

ARIES

PISCES

TAURUS

ERIDANUS

CETUS

Mira

W

February – Looking North

The months of January and February are probably the best time for seeing the section of the Milky Way that runs in the northern and western sky from **Cygnus**, low on the northern horizon, through **Cassiopeia**, **Perseus** and **Auriga** and then down through **Gemini** and **Orion**. Although not as readily visible as the denser star clouds of the summer Milky Way, on a clear night so many stars may be seen that even a distinctive constellation such as **Cassiopeia** is not immediately obvious.

The head of **Draco** is now higher in the sky and easier to recognize. **Deneb** (α Cygni), the brightest star in **Cygnus**, may just be visible almost due north at midnight, early in the month, if the sky is very clear and the horizon clear of obstacles. **Vega** (α Lyrae) in **Lyra** is so low that it is difficult to see, but may become visible later in the night. The constellation of **Boötes** – sometimes described as shaped like a kite, an ice-cream cone, or the letter 'P' – with orange-tinted **Arcturus** (α Boötis), is beginning to clear the eastern horizon. Arcturus, at magnitude -0.05, is the brightest star in the northern hemisphere of the sky. The inconspicuous constellation of **Coma Berenices** is now well above the horizon in the east. The concentration of faint stars at the northwestern corner somewhat resembles a tiny, detached portion of the Milky Way. This is Melotte 111, an open star cluster (which is sometimes called the Coma Cluster, but must not be confused with the important Coma Cluster of galaxies, Abell 1656, mentioned on page 55).

On the other side of the sky, in the northwest, most of the constellation of **Andromeda** is still easily seen, although **Alpheratz** (α Andromedae), the star that forms the northeastern corner of the Great Square of Pegasus – even though it is actually part of Andromeda – is becoming close to the horizon and more difficult to detect. High overhead, at the zenith, try to make out the very faint constellation of **Lynx**. It was introduced in 1687 by the famous astronomer Johannes Hevelius to fill the largely blank area between **Auriga**, **Gemini** and **Ursa Major**, and is reputed to be so named because one needed the eyes of a lynx to detect it.

A very large, and frequently ignored, open star cluster, Melotte 111, also known as the Coma Cluster, is readily visible in the eastern sky during February.

February 01   23:00 GMT
February 15   22:00 GMT

February – Looking South

Apart from **Orion**, the most prominent constellation visible this month is **Gemini**, with its two lines of stars running southwest towards **Orion**. Many people have difficulty in remembering which is which of the two stars **Castor** and **Pollux**. Castor (α Geminorum), the fainter star (mag. 1.9), is closer to the North Celestial Pole. Pollux (β Geminorum) is the brighter of the two (mag. 1.2), but is farther away from the Pole. Pollux is one of the first-magnitude stars that may be occulted by the Moon. Castor is remarkable because it is actually a multiple system, consisting of no less than six individual stars.

Orion's belt points down to the southeast towards **Sirius**, the brightest star in the sky (at magnitude -1.4) in the constellation of **Canis Major**, the whole of which is now clear of the southern horizon. Forming an equilateral triangle with **Betelgeuse** in **Orion** and **Sirius** in Canis Major is **Procyon**, the brightest star in the small constellation of **Canis Minor**. Between Canis Major and Canis Minor is the faint constellation of **Monoceros**, which actually straddles the Milky Way, which, although faint, has many clusters in this area. Directly east of Procyon is the highly distinctive asterism of six stars that form the

The constellation of Gemini. The two brightest stars, visible on the left-hand side of the photograph, are Castor and Pollux.

'head' of **Hydra**, the largest of all 88 constellations, and which trails such a long way across the sky that it is only in mid-March around midnight that the whole constellation becomes visible.

The Moon's phases for February

February – Moon and Planets

The Moon

On February 3, just after midnight one day before Last Quarter, the Moon passes 6.8° north of **Spica** in **Virgo**. On February 6 it is 5.4° north of **Antares** in **Scorpius**. On February 18 it passes 3.7° south of **Mars**. Two days later, it passes south of the **Pleiades** and then 5.0° north of **Aldebaran** in **Taurus**. On January 24 it is 3.7°S of **Pollux**, and on February 26, 4.6°N of **Regulus** in **Leo**.

Occultations

Of the bright stars near the ecliptic that may be occulted by the Moon (**Aldebaran**, **Antares**, **Pollux**, **Regulus** and **Spica**), none are occulted in 2021. There is one occultation of **Mars**, on April 17, partly visible from Southeast Asia.

The planets

Mercury passes inferior conjunction on February 8. **Venus** is invisible in the morning twilight. **Mars**, fading from mag. 0.4 to 0.9, moves eastwards from **Aries** into **Taurus**. **Jupiter** remains too close to the Sun to be visible. **Saturn** is also lost in morning twilight. **Uranus** (mag. 5.8) is in **Aries** and **Neptune** (mag. 7.9 to 8.0) remains in **Aquarius**.

The path of the Sun and the planets along the ecliptic in February.

Calendar for February

03	00:02	Spica 6.8°S of Moon
03	19:03	Moon at perigee (370,127 km)
04	17:37	Last Quarter
06	05:00 *	Saturn 0.4°N of Venus
06	09:04	Antares 5.4°S of Moon
08	13:48	Mercury at inferior conjunction
10	11:10	Saturn 3.4°N of Moon
10	20:25	Venus 3.2°N of Moon
10	21:35	Jupiter 3.7°N of Moon
11	03:17	Mercury 8.3°N of Moon
11	12:00 *	Jupiter 0.4°N of Venus
11	19:06	New Moon
12	17:00 *	Mercury 4.8°N of Venus
13	16:57	Neptune 4.3°N of Moon
13	19:00 *	Mercury 4.2°N of Jupiter
17	15:48	Uranus 3.0°N of Moon
18	10:22	Moon at apogee (404,467 km)
18	22:46	Mars 3.7°N of Moon
19	18:47	First Quarter
20	13:50	Aldebaran 5.0°S of Moon
24	01:42	Pollux 3.7°N of Moon
26	14:33	Regulus 4.6°S of Moon
27	08:17	Full Moon

These objects are close together for an extended period around this time.

Morning 6:30

February 6 • *In the early morning, the waning crescent Moon is five degrees north of Antares. Sabik is farther southeast.*

Evening 23:00

February 18–20 • *The First Quarter Moon passes Mars, the Pleiades and Aldebaran in the west. Mars (mag. 0.7) is just slightly brighter than Aldebaran (mag. 0.9).*

Early morning 3:00

February 24 • *The Moon with Castor and Pollux in the western sky, in the early morning. Procyon and Alhena are close to the horizon.*

Evening 18:30

February 26 • *The Moon is almost full when it passes between Regulus and Algieba. Denebola (mag. 2.1) is probably too low to be easily detected.*

March – Looking North

In March, the Sun crosses the celestial equator on Saturday, March 20, at the vernal equinox, when day and night are of almost exactly equal length, and the northern season of spring is considered to begin. (The hours of daylight and darkness change most rapidly around the equinoxes, in March and September.) It is also in March that Summer Time begins in Europe (on Sunday, March 28) so the charts show the appearance at 23:00 GMT for March 1 and 22:00 BST for April 1. (In North America, Daylight Saving Time is introduced two weeks earlier, on Sunday, March 14.)

Early in the month, the constellation of **Cepheus** lies almost due north, with the distinctive 'W' of **Cassiopeia** to its west. Cepheus lies across the border of the Milky Way and is often described as like the gable-end of a house or a church tower and steeple. Despite the large number of stars revealed at the base of the constellation by binoculars, one star stands out because of its deep red colour. This is **μ Cephei**, also known as the Garnet Star, a red supergiant, and one of the largest stars known. It is about 2400 times the diameter of the Sun, and if placed in the Solar System would extend beyond the orbit of Saturn. (Betelgeuse, in Orion, is also a red supergiant, but it is 'only' about 500 times the diameter of the Sun.)

Another famous, and very important star in Cepheus is **δ Cephei**, which is the prototype for the class of variable stars known as Cepheids. These giant stars show a regular variation in their luminosity, and there is a direct relationship between the period of the changes in magnitude and the stars' actual luminosity. From a knowledge of the period of any Cepheid, its actual luminosity – known as its absolute magnitude – may be derived. A comparison of its apparent magnitude on the sky and its absolute magnitude enables the star's exact distance to be

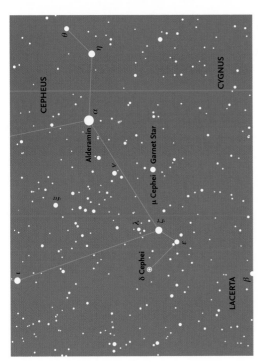

A finder chart for δ Cephei and μ Cephei (the Garnet Star). All stars brighter than magnitude 7.5 are shown.

determined. Once the distances to the first Cepheid variables had been established, examples in more distant galaxies provided information about the scale of the universe. Cepheid variables are the first 'rung' in the cosmic distance ladder. Both important stars are shown on the accompanying chart and in the photograph on page 49.

Below Cepheus to the east (to the right), it may be possible to catch a glimpse of **Deneb** (α Cygni), just above the horizon. Slightly farther round towards the northeast, **Vega** (α Lyrae) is marginally higher in the sky. From southern Britain, Deneb is just far enough north to be circumpolar (although difficult to see in January and February because it is so low on the northern horizon). Vega, by contrast, farther south, is completely hidden during the depths of winter.

March 01   23:00 GMT
March 15   22:00 GMT

March – Looking South

Due south at 22:00 at the beginning of the month, lying between the constellations of **Gemini** in the west and **Leo** in the east, and fairly high in the sky above the head of **Hydra**, is the faint, and rather undistinguished zodiacal constellation of **Cancer**. Rather like the triskelion, the symbol for the Isle of Man, it has three 'legs' radiating from the centre, where there is an open cluster, M44 or **Praesepe** ('the Manger' but also known as 'the Beehive'). On a clear night this cluster, known since antiquity, is just a hazy spot to the naked eye, but appears in binoculars as a group of dozens of individual stars.

Also prominent in March is the constellation of **Leo,** with the 'backward question mark' (or 'Sickle') of bright stars forming the head of the mythological lion. **Regulus** (α Leonis) – the 'dot' of the 'question mark' or the handle of the sickle and the brightest star in Leo – lies very close to the ecliptic and is one of the few first-magnitude stars that may be occulted by the Moon. However, there are no occultations of Regulus in 2021, nor of any of the other four bright stars near the ecliptic.

The constellation of Cepheus. The locations of both δ and μ Cephei are shown on the chart on page 47. The bright star near the left edge of the image is Caph (β Cas).

The Moon's phases for March

							Last Quarter							New Moon	
01	02	03	04	05	06 01:30	07	08	09	10	11	12	13 10:21	14	15	16
Day 18	Day 19	Day 20	Day 21	Day 22	Day 23	Day 24	Day 25	Day 26	Day 27	Day 28	Day 29	Day 1	Day 2	Day 3	Day 4

				First Quarter							Full Moon				
17	18	19	20	21 14:40	22	23	24	25	26	27	28 18:48	29	30	31	
Day 5	Day 6	Day 7	Day 8	Day 9	Day 10	Day 11	Day 12	Day 13	Day 14	Day 15	Day 16	Day 17	Day 18	Day 19	

March – Moon and Planets

The Moon

On March 2, the Moon is 6.6° north of *Spica* in *Virgo*. On March 5, just before Last Quarter, the Moon is 5.2° north of *Antares* in *Scorpius*. On March 19, the Moon passes south of the *Pleiades* and *Mars* and north of *Aldebaran* in *Taurus*. On March 23, the Moon is 3.5° south of *Pollux* in *Gemini*. On March 26 it is 4.7° north of *Regulus* in *Leo*.

The Planets

On March 6, *Mercury* is at greatest western elongation 27.3° away from the Sun, low in morning twilight. *Venus* is also invisible in the twilight as it moves from the morning to the evening sky. It is at superior conjunction on March 26. During the month, *Mars* brightens slightly from mag. 0.9 to 1.3 as it moves eastwards in *Taurus*. *Jupiter* is in the morning twilight in *Capricornus* as is *Saturn*. Uranus (mag. 5.8) is in *Pisces*, close to the Sun. *Neptune* remains in *Aquarius*, also close to the Sun, passing superior conjunction on March 11. Minor planet (4) *Vesta* comes to opposition in *Leo* at mag. 0.6 on March 4, (see chart on page 26).

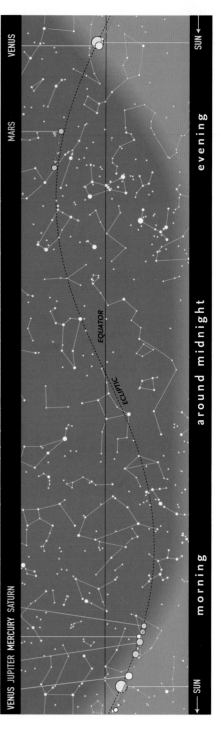

The path of the Sun and the planets along the ecliptic in March.

* These objects are close together for an extended
_riod around this time.

Early morning 4:00

March 5–6 • The Moon passes between Antares and
Sabik, low in the south-southeast. Last Quarter Moon
is on March 6, just a few hours earlier (1:30).

Evening 19:00

March 22–23 • The Moon passes Castor and Pollux
high in the south-southeast. Alhena (γ Gem) and
Procyon are also nearby.

Evening 22:00

March 19 • The Moon is between Mars (mag. 1.1) and
Aldebaran (mag. 0.9) in the western sky. The Pleiades
are a little farther to the northwest.

Evening 19:00

March 25–26 • The Moon passes between Regulus and
Algieba, in the constellation of Leo. Denebola (mag.
2 ') is only slightly fainter than Algieba (mag. 1.9)

April – Looking North

Cygnus and the brighter regions of the Milky Way are now becoming visible, running more-or-less parallel with the horizon in the early part of the night. Rising in the northeast is the small constellation of **Lyra** and the distinctive 'Keystone' of **Hercules** above it. This asterism is very useful for locating the bright globular cluster M13 (see map on page 59), which lies on one side of the quadrilateral. The winding constellation of **Draco** weaves its way from the four stars that mark its 'head', on the border with Hercules, to end at **Giausar** (λ Draconis) between **Polaris** (α Ursae Minoris) and the 'Pointers', **Dubhe** and **Merak** (α and β Ursae Majoris, respectively). **Ursa Major** is 'upside down' high overhead, near the zenith. The constellation of **Gemini** stands almost vertically in the west. **Auriga** is still clearly seen in the northwest, but, by the end of the month, the southern portion of **Perseus** is starting to dip below the northern horizon. The very faint constellation of **Camelopardalis** lies in the northwest between Polaris and the constellations of Auriga and Perseus.

Meteors

A moderate meteor shower, the **Lyrids**, peaks on April 22–23. Although the hourly rate is not very high (about 18 meteors per hour), the meteors are fast and some leave persistent trains. This year the maximum occurs when the Moon is waxing gibbous, four days before Full Moon, so there will be considerable interference from moonlight. The parent object is the non-periodic comet C/1861 G1 (Thatcher). Another, stronger shower, the **η-Aquariids**, begins to be active around April 18 (with a waxing crescent Moon) and comes to maximum in early May.

The constellation of Draco, winding round Ursa Minor, with Polaris centre left.

April 01   00:00 BST (GMT + 1hr)
April 15   23:00 BST (GMT + 1hr)

TAURUS
Elnath
AURIGA
Capella
The Kids
MARS
ORION
M35
GEMINI
Betelgeuse
Castor
Pollux
Alhena
MONOCEROS
LYNX
CANCER
CANIS MINOR
M44
Praesepe
Procyon
M67
URSA MAJOR
LEO MINOR
PUPPIS
Algieba
Alphard
HYDRA
SEXTANS
Regulus
LEO
PYXIS
ZENITH
The Plough
ECLIPTIC
Ghost of Jupiter
ANTLIA
Melotte 111
CANES VENATICI
COMA BERENICES
Denebola
CRATER
S
DRACO
M3
BOÖTES
VIRGO
CORVUS
CENTAURUS
Vega
Arcturus
Spica
HYDRA
M13
Alphecca
CORONA BOREALIS
LIBRA
M57
Ring Nebula
Keystone
HERCULES
SERPENS CAPUT
April Lyrids
LYRA
CYGNUS
OPHIUCHUS
E

April – Looking South

Leo is the most prominent constellation in the southern sky in April, and vaguely looks like the creature after which it is named. **Gemini**, with **Castor** and **Pollux**, remains clearly visible in the west, and **Cancer** lies between the two constellations. To the east of Leo, the whole of **Virgo**, with **Spica** (α Virginis) its brightest star, is well clear of the horizon. Below Leo and Virgo, the complete length of **Hydra** is visible, running beneath both constellations, with **Alphard** (α Hydrae) halfway between Regulus and the southwestern horizon. Farther east, the two small constellations of **Crater** and the rather brighter **Corvus** lie between Hydra and Virgo.

Boötes and **Arcturus** are prominent in the eastern sky, together with the circlet of **Corona Borealis**, framed by Boötes and the neighbouring constellation of **Hercules**. Between Leo and Boötes lies the constellation of **Coma Berenices**, notable for being the location of the open cluster Melotte 111 (see page 41) and the Coma Cluster of galaxies (Abell 1656). There are about 1000 galaxies in this cluster, which is located near the North Galactic Pole, where we are looking out of the plane of the Galaxy and are thus able to see deep into space. Only about ten of the brightest galaxies in the Coma Cluster are visible with the largest amateur telescopes.

The distinctive constellation of Leo, with Regulus and 'The Sickle' on the west. Algieba (γ Leonis), north of Regulus, appearing double, is a multiple system of four stars.

The Moon's phases for April

				Last Quarter				
01	02	03	04 10:02	05	06	07	08	
Day 20	Day 21	Day 22	Day 23	Day 24	Day 25	Day 26	Day 27	

New Moon
Full Moon
First Quarter

April – Moon and Planets

The Moon

On April 1, the waning gibbous Moon is north of **Antares**. On April 6–7, a waning crescent, it passes south of **Saturn** and **Jupiter** in the morning sky. On April 16–17, the waxing crescent Moon passes the **Pleiades**, **Aldebaran** and **Mars**. It passes 0.1° north of Mars on April 17, and there is an occultation, but the end (reappearance) only is visible from southern Asia. On April 19, the Moon (a day before First Quarter), passes 3.2° south of **Pollux** in **Gemini**. The Moon is 6.5° north of **Spica** in **Virgo** on April 26 and 4.8°N of **Antares** in **Scorpius** on April 29.

The planets

Mercury is close to the Sun and comes to superior conjunction on April 19. **Venus** is lost in twilight, it is initially in the morning sky, but moves into the evening later in the month. **Mars** (fading slightly from mag. 1.3 to 1.5) moves from **Taurus** into **Gemini** late in the month. **Jupiter** (mag. -2.1 to -2.2) moves slowly east in the morning sky, entering **Aquarius** at the very end of the month. **Saturn** (also in the morning sky) brightens very slightly from mag. 0.8 to 0.7 and is in **Capricornus**. **Uranus** is in conjunction with the Sun on April 30, in **Aries**, while **Neptune** (mag. 8.0 to 7.9) is in **Aquarius**.

The path of the Sun and the planets along the ecliptic in April.

Evening 21:00 (BST)

April 15–17 • *The waxing crescent Moon passes Aldebaran, Elnath and Mars, high in the west. Mars has now faded to magnitude 1.4.*

Early morning 5:45 (BST)

pril 6–7 • *The waning crescent Moon passes Saturn nd Jupiter very low in the southeast and shortly before unrise.*

Morning 5:00 (BST)

April 29 • *In the early morning, the Moon is in the company of Antares, near the south southwest, with*

Evening 23:00 (BST)

April 19 • *In the western sky, the Moon lines up with astor and Pollux. Procyon and Alhena are closer to*

SERPENS
CAUDA

SO

AQUILA

Altair

SAGITTA

DELPHINUS

M57
Ring Nebula

M27
Dumbbell Nebula

Rasalgethi

VULPECULA

Keystone

LYRA

CYGNUS

PEGASUS

Vega

M13

HERCULES

Deneb

CORONA
BOREALIS

LACERTA

CEPHEUS

Caph

Andromeda Galaxy
M31

DRACO

CASSIOPEIA

Alkaid

ZENITH

URSA MINOR

Double Cluster

N

CANES VENATICI

The Plough

Polaris

ANDROMEDA

AMELOPARDALIS

Algol

May – Looking North

Cassiopeia is now low over the northern horizon and, to its west, the southern portions of both **Perseus** and **Auriga** are becoming difficult to observe, although the **Double Cluster**, between Perseus and Cassiopeia is still clearly visible. The **Andromeda Galaxy** is now too low to be readily visible. The constellations of **Lyra**, **Cepheus**, **Ursa Minor** and the whole of **Draco** are well placed in the sky. **Gemini**, with **Castor** and **Pollux**, is sinking towards the western horizon. **Capella** (α Aurigae) and the asterism of **The Kids** are still clear of the horizon.

In the east, two of the stars of the 'Summer Triangle', **Vega** (α Lyrae) and **Deneb** (α Cygni), are clearly visible, and the third star, **Altair** in **Aquila**, is beginning to climb above the horizon. The whole of **Cygnus** is now visible. The sprawling constellation of **Hercules** is high in the east and the brightest globular cluster in the northern hemisphere, M13, is visible to the naked eye on the western side of the asterism known as the **Keystone**.

Three faint constellations may be identified before the lighter nights of summer make them difficult objects. Below Cepheus, in the northeastern sky is the zig-zag constellation of **Lacerta**, while to the west, above Perseus and Auriga is **Camelopardalis** and, farther west, the line of faint stars forming **Lynx**.

Later in the night (and in the month) the westernmost stars of **Pegasus** begin to come into view, while the stars of **Andromeda** are skimming the northeastern horizon and the Andromeda Galaxy may become visible. High overhead, **Alkaid** (η Ursae Majoris), the last star in the 'tail' of the Great Bear, is close to the zenith, while the main body of the constellation has swung round into the western sky.

Meteors

The **η-Aquariids** are one of the two meteor showers associated with Comet 1P/Halley (the other being the **Orionids**, in October). The **η-Aquariids** are not particularly favourably placed for northern-

hemisphere observers, because the radiant is near the celestial equator, near the 'Water Jar' in **Aquarius**, well below the horizon until late in the night (around dawn). However, meteors may still be seen in the eastern sky even when the radiant is below the horizon. There is a radiant map for the η-Aquariids on page 30.

Their maximum in 2021, on May 6, occurs when the Moon is a waning crescent, a few days after Last Quarter, so conditions are reasonably favourable. Maximum hourly rate is about 40 per hour and a large proportion (about 25 per cent) of the meteors leave persistent trains.

Finder chart for M13, the finest globular cluster in the northern sky. All stars down to magnitude 7.5 are shown.

May · Looking South

May 01 — 00:00 BST (GMT + 1hr)
May 15 — 23:00 BST (GMT + 1hr)
June 01 — 22:00 BST (GMT + 1hr)

May – Looking South

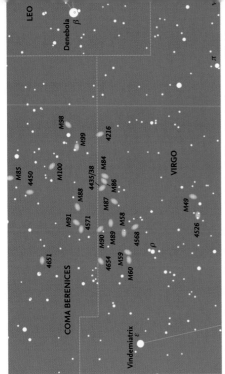

Early in the night, the constellation of **Virgo**, with **Spica** (α Virginis), lies due south, with **Leo** and both **Regulus** and **Denebola** (α and β Leonis, respectively) to its west still well clear of the horizon. Later in the night, the rather faint zodiacal constellation of **Libra** becomes visible and, to its east, the ruddy star **Antares** (α Scorpii) begins to climb up over the horizon.

Virgo contains the nearest large cluster of galaxies, which is the centre of the Local Supercluster, of which the Milky Way galaxy forms part. The Virgo Cluster contains some 2000 galaxies, the brightest of which are visible in amateur telescopes.

Arcturus in **Boötes** is high in the south, with the distinctive circlet of **Corona Borealis** clearly visible to its east. The brightest star (α Coronae Borealis) is known as **Alphecca**. The large constellation of **Ophiuchus** (which actually crosses the ecliptic, and is thus the 'thirteenth' zodiacal constellation) is climbing into the eastern sky. Before the constellation boundaries were formally adopted by the International Astronomical Union in 1930, the southern region of Ophiuchus was regarded as forming part of the constellation of Scorpius, which had been part of the zodiac since antiquity.

The Moon's phases for May

A finder chart for some of the brightest galaxies in the Virgo Cluster (see page 60). All stars brighter than magnitude 8.5 are shown.

May – Moon and Planets

The Moon

The Moon is at its most distant apogee of the year (406,512 km) on May 11. On May 3, just before Last Quarter, the Moon is 4.2° south of *Saturn*, in *Capricornus*, and one day later it passes 4.6° south of *Jupiter* in *Aquarius*. On May 12–13, the Moon (immediately after New Moon, as a narrow waxing crescent) passes *Venus*, *Aldebaran* and then *Mercury*. A few days later (May 16–17) the Moon is visible 1.5° north of *Mars* in *Gemini* and then 3.1° south of *Pollux*. On May 19, the Moon passes between *Regulus* and *Algieba* (γ Leonis) in *Leo*. On May 23, waxing gibbous, the Moon is 6.5° north of *Spica*, and on May 26 (at Full Moon) there is a total lunar eclipse, visible from the Americas, the Pacific, Australia and parts of Asia. By May 30, the Moon is again south of *Saturn* in *Capricornus*.

The planets

Mercury is at greatest elongation east (22°) in the evening sky at mag. 0.3 on May 17. *Venus* (which passed superior conjunction in March), becomes visible for a brief period low in the evening sky at mag. -3.9. *Mars* (mag. 1.6–1.7) crosses *Gemini* over the month. *Jupiter* (mag. -2.2 to -2.4) is in *Aquarius*. *Saturn* (mag. 0.7–0.6) in *Capricornus* begins retrograde motion on May 24. *Uranus* (mag. 5.9) is in *Aries* and *Neptune* in *Aquarius* at mag. 7.9.

The path of the Sun and the planets along the ecliptic in May.

Calendar for May

03	16:58	Saturn 4.2°N of Moon
03	19:50	Last Quarter
04	21:02	Jupiter 4.6°N of Moon
06		η-Aquariid shower maximum
06	17:51	Neptune 4.4°N of Moon
10	21:06	Uranus 2.4°N of Moon
11	19:00	New Moon
11	21:53	Moon at apogee (406,512 km, greatest of year)
12	22:03	Venus 0.7°N of Moon
13	10:48	Aldebaran 5.5°S of Moon
13	17:59	Mercury 2.1°N of Moon
16	04:47	Mars 1.5°S of Moon
17	01:12	Pollux 3.1°N of Moon
17	05:54	Mercury at greatest elongation (22.0°E, mag. 0.3)
17	23:00 *	Venus 5.9°N of Aldebaran
19	17:59	Regulus 5.0°S of Moon
19	19:13	First Quarter
23	13:38	Spica 6.5°S of Moon
26	01:50	Moon at perigee (357,311 km)
26	11:14	Full Moon
26	11:18	Total lunar eclipse (Americas, Pacific, Australia, Asia)
26	17:25	Antares 4.8°S of Moon
29	06:00 *	Mercury 0.4°S of Venus
31	01:18	Saturn 4.2°N of Moon

* These objects are close together for an extended period around this time.

Early morning 4:30 (BST)

May 3–5 • The Moon is around Last Quarter when it passes Saturn and Jupiter, very low in the southeast.

Evening 21:10 (BST)

May 12–13 • After sunset, the narrow crescent Moon passes Venus and Mercury, very low in the west-northwest.

Evening 22:00 (BST)

May 15–17 • The Moon passes Mars, Castor and Pollux in the western sky. Mars has now faded to magnitude 1.6. Procyon and Alhena are closer to the horizon.

Evening 22:00 (BST)

May 19 • The Moon is between Regulus and Algieba, high in the southwest.

June – Looking North

00:00 BST (GMT + 1hr)   June 01
23:00 BST (GMT + 1hr)   June 15
22:00 BST (GMT + 1hr)   July 01

June – Looking North

Around summer solstice (June 21) even in southern England and Ireland a form of twilight persists throughout the night. Farther north, in Scotland, the sky remains so light that most of the fainter stars and constellations are invisible. There, even brighter stars, such as the seven stars making up the well-known asterism known as the *Plough* in *Ursa Major* may be difficult to detect except around local midnight, 00:00 UT (01:00 BST).

But there is one compensation during these light nights: even southern observers may be lucky enough to witness a display of noctilucent clouds (NLC). These are highly distinctive clouds shining with an electric-blue tint, observed in the sky in the direction of the North Pole. They are the highest clouds in the atmosphere, occurring at altitudes of 80–85 km, far above all other clouds. They are only visible during summer nights, for about a month or six weeks on either side of the solstice, when observers are in darkness, but the clouds themselves remain illuminated by sunlight, reaching them from the Sun, itself hidden below the northern horizon.

Noctilucent clouds, photographed on the night of 5–6 July 2016, from Tarbatness, Ross-shire, Scotland, by Denis Buczynski.

June – Looking South

June – Looking South

Although the persistent twilight makes observing even the southern sky difficult, the rather undistinguished constellation of *Libra* lies almost due south. The red supergiant star **Antares** – the name means the 'Rival of Mars' – in **Scorpius** is visible slightly to the east of the meridian, but the 'tail' or 'sting' remains below the horizon. Higher in the sky is the large constellation of **Ophiuchus** (the 'Serpent Bearer'), lying between the two halves of the constellation of **Serpens: Serpens Caput** ('Head of the Serpent') to the west and **Serpens Cauda** ('Tail of the Serpent') to the east. (Serpens is the only constellation to be divided into two distinct parts.) The ecliptic runs across Ophiuchus, and the Sun actually spends far more time in the constellation than it does in the 'classical' zodiacal constellation of Scorpius, a small area of which lies between Libra and Ophiuchus.

Higher in the southern sky, the three constellations of **Boötes, Corona Borealis** and **Hercules** are now better placed for observation than at any other time of the year. This is an ideal time to observe the fine globular cluster of M13 in Hercules (see finder chart on page 59).

The Moon's phases for June

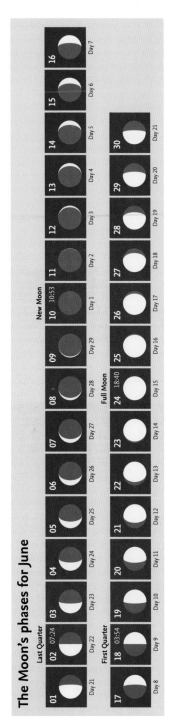

The constellations of Boötes and Corona Borealis are high in the sky in June. Arcturus has an orange tint and is the brightest star in the northern celestial hemisphere.

June – Moon and Planets

The Moon

One June 1, the day before Last Quarter, the Moon is 4.6° south of *Jupiter* in *Aquarius*. On June 10, at New Moon, there is an annular solar eclipse, visible from the high latitudes of Arctic Canada and Greenland (see page 20). On June 12–13, the Moon passes *Venus* and *Pollux* in *Gemini* and then 2.8° north of *Mars*. On June 15, the Moon is 5.0° north of *Regulus* in *Leo* and on June 19 it is close to *Spica* in *Virgo* as it sets in the west. On June 27 it passes, first 4.0° south of *Saturn* in *Capricornus* and then (on June 28), 4.5° south of *Jupiter* in *Aquarius*.

The planets

Mercury is invisible in twilight close to the Sun as it passes inferior conjunction on June 11. *Venus* is mag. -3.8, very close to the Sun, but may perhaps be glimpsed in the twilight at the end of the month. On June 22, it is south of *Pollux* and in the same field as Mars. At Last Quarter Moon, on June 2, *Mars* is 5.4° south of Pollux in *Gemini*. During the month, it moves from Gemini into *Cancer*, where it crosses the open cluster *Praesepe* on June 22 to 25 (see chart on page 23). *Jupiter*, in *Aquarius* (mag. -2.4 to -2.6) begins retrograde motion on June 21. *Saturn* (mag. 0.6–0.4) is moving westwards (retrograde) in Capricornus. *Uranus* (mag. 5.9–5.8) is in *Aries* and *Neptune* (mag. 7.9), in *Aquarius*, close to the border of *Pisces*, begins slow retrograde motion on June 27.

The path of the Sun and the planets along the ecliptic in June.

Calendar for June

01	09:00	Jupiter 4.6°N of Moon
02	07:24	Last Quarter
02	14:00 *	Mars 5.4°S of Pollux
03	01:06	Neptune 4.5°N of Moon
07	06:16	Uranus 2.3°N of Moon
08	02:27	Moon at apogee (406,228 km)
09	16:51	Aldebaran 5.5°S of Moon
10	10:41	Annular solar eclipse (Arctic Canada, Greenland)
10	10:53	New Moon
10	13:09	Mercury 4.0°S of Moon
11	01:13	Mercury at inferior conjunction
12	06:42	Venus 1.5°S of Moon
13	06:52	Pollux 3.1°N of Moon
13	19:52	Mars 2.8°S of Moon
15	23:59	Regulus 5.0°S of Moon
18	03:54	First Quarter
19	22:09	Spica 6.5°S of Moon
21	03:32	Summer solstice
22	15:00 *	Venus 5.3°S of Pollux
23	03:56	Antares 4.8°S of Moon
23	09:55	Moon at perigee (359,956 km)
24	18:40	Full Moon
27	09:27	Saturn 4.0°N of Moon
28	18:42	Jupiter 4.5°N of Moon
30	09:09	Neptune 4.4°N of Moon

* These objects are close together for an extended period around this time.

Evening 22:00 (BST)

June 2 • Mars with Castor and Pollux in the north-northwest. Mars has now faded to magnitude 1.7 (slightly fainter than Castor).

Evening 22:15 (BST)

June 22 • Venus with Castor and Pollux, close to the northwestern horizon. Mars (now at mag. 1.8) is a little farther to the west.

Evening 22:15 (BST)

June 12–13 • The narrow crescent Moon passes Castor, Pollux and Mars, after sunset, low in the west-northwest. Venus is nearby and closer to the horizon.

Early morning 4:00 (BST)

June 27–29 • The Moon passes Saturn and Jupiter in the early morning, almost due south. Fomalhaut is close to the horizon.

ECLIPTIC
CAPRICORNUS
JUPITER
AQUARIUS
PISCES
E

EQUULEUS
M15
PEGASUS
Great Square
of Pegasus
ANDROMEDA
Alpheratz
PISCES
DELPHINUS
Andromeda Galaxy
M31
TRIANGULUM
NGC 752
SAGITTA
M27
Dumbbell Nebula
LACERTA
CEPHEUS
Caph
Double Cluster
Algol
PERSEUS
Deneb
CASSIOPEIA
VULPECULA
M57 Ring Nebula
Albireo
CYGNUS
LYRA
Vega
CAMELOPARDALIS
Capella
HERCULES
Keystone
ZENITH
DRACO
URSA MINOR
Polaris
N
AURIGA
M13
CORONA
BOREALIS
LYNX
Alphecca
SERPENS CAPUT
The Plough
CANES VENATICI
URSA
MAJOR
LEO MINOR
BOÖTES
M3
Arcturus
COMA
BERENICES
Melotte 111
Denebola
Algieba
LEO
VIRGO
Spica
ECLIPTIC
W

July – Looking North

As in June, light nights and the chance of observing noctilucent clouds persist throughout July, but later in the month (and particularly after midnight) some of the major constellations begin to be more easily seen. **Capella**, the brightest star in **Auriga** (most of which is too low to be visible), is skimming the northern horizon. **Cassiopeia** is clearly visible in the northeast and **Perseus**, to its south, is beginning to climb clear of the horizon. The band of the Milky Way, from Perseus through Cassiopeia towards **Cygnus**, stretches up into the northeastern sky. If the sky is dark and clear, you may be able to make out the small, faint constellation of **Lacerta**, lying across the Milky Way between Cassiopeia and Cygnus. In the east, the stars of **Pegasus** are now well clear of the horizon, with the main line of stars forming **Andromeda** roughly parallel to the horizon in the northeast. **Alpheratz** (α Andromedae) is actually the star at the northeastern corner of the **Great Square of Pegasus**. **Cepheus** and **Ursa Major** are on opposite sides of **Polaris** and **Ursa Minor**, in the east and west, respectively. The head of **Draco** is very close to the zenith so the whole of this winding constellation is readily seen.

Meteors

July brings increasing meteor activity, mainly because there are several minor radiants active in the constellations of **Capricornus** and **Aquarius**. Because of their location, however, observing conditions are not particularly favourable for northern-hemisphere observers, although the first shower, the **α-Capricornids**, active from July 2 to August 14 (peaking July 30, with a tail to August 14), does often produce very bright fireballs. The maximum rate, however, is only about 5 per hour. The parent body is Comet 169P/NEAT. The most prominent shower is probably that of the **Southern δ-Aquariids**, which are active from around July 13 to August 24, with a peak on July 30, although even then the rate is unlikely to reach 25 meteors per hour. In this case,

Cygnus, sometimes known as the 'Northern Cross', depicts a swan 'flying' down the Milky Way towards Sagittarius. The brightest star, Deneb (α Cygni), represents the tail, and Albireo (β Cygni) marks the position of the head, and lies near the bottom of the image.

the parent body may be Comet 96P/Machholz. This year, both shower maxima occur when the Moon is a waning gibbous, so observing conditions are not particularly favourable. A chart showing the δ-Aquariids radiant is shown on page 30. The **Perseids** begin on July 16 and peak on August 12–13.

July – Looking South

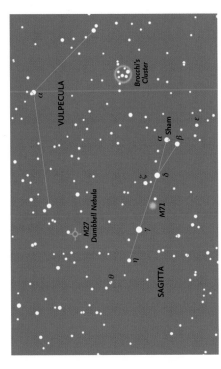

Although part of the constellation remains hidden, this is perhaps the best time of year to see **Scorpius**, with deep red **Antares** (α Scorpii), glowing just above the southern horizon. At around midnight (UT), 01:00 BST, part of **Sagittarius**, with the distinctive asterism of the 'Teapot', and the dense star clouds of the centre of the Milky Way, are just visible in the south. The **Great Rift** – actually dust clouds that hide the more distant stars – runs down the Milky Way from Cygnus towards Sagittarius. Towards its northern end is the small constellation of **Sagitta** and the planetary nebula **M27** (the Dumbbell Nebula) in the otherwise insignificant constellation of **Vulpecula**. The sprawling constellation of **Ophiuchus** lies close to the meridian for a large part of the month, separating the two halves of the constellation of **Serpens**. The western half is called **Serpens Caput** (Head of the Serpent) and the eastern part **Serpens Cauda** (Tail of the Serpent). In the east, the bright **Summer Triangle**, consisting of **Vega** in **Lyra**, **Deneb** in **Cygnus** and **Altair** in **Aquila**, begins to dominate the southern sky, as it will throughout August and into September. The small constellation of Lyra, with Vega and a distinctive quadrilateral of stars to its east and south, lies not far south of the zenith.

A finder chart for M27, the Dumbbell Nebula, a relatively bright (magnitude 8) planetary nebula – a shell of material ejected in the late stages of a star's lifetime – in the constellation of Vulpecula. All stars brighter than magnitude 7.5 are shown.

The Moon's phases for July

July – Moon and Planets

The Earth

The Earth reaches aphelion, farthest from the Sun in its yearly orbit, at 22:27 on July 5, at a distance of 1.016729224 AU (152,100,527 km).

The Moon

The Moon is 5.6° north of **Aldebaran** in **Taurus** on July 6 and then passes between **Elnath** (β Tauri) and **Mercury**, which is low in the morning sky, on July 8. On July 12, the Moon passes north of **Venus** and **Mars** and then, on July 13, between **Regulus** and **Algieba** (γ Leonis). On July 17, at First Quarter, the Moon is 6.4° north of **Spica** in **Virgo**. On July 20, it passes 4.7° north of **Saturn**. At Full Moon on July 24, the Moon is just 3.8° south of **Saturn**, very low in the south. The next day, July 25, the Moon is southwest of **Jupiter** and passes 4.2° south of the planet on July 26.

The planets

Mercury is at greatest western elongation (21.6°) low in the morning sky on July 4. It rapidly moves towards the Sun to superior conjunction in August. **Venus** is bright (mag. -3.9) but generally low in the evening sky. It leaves **Cancer**, entering **Leo**, and passes Mars in the middle of the month. **Mars**, in Leo, is not very bright (mag. 1.8) and is also low in the evening sky. **Jupiter** (mag. -2.6 to -2.8) is slowly retrograding in **Aquarius**. **Saturn** (mag. 0.4 to 0.2) is also slowly retrograding, in **Aquarius**. **Uranus** (mag. 5.8) is moving slowly eastwards in **Aries** and **Capricornus**. **Neptune** (mag. 7.8 to 7.9) is retrograding very slowly in **Aquarius**, near the border of **Pisces**. The minor planet **(6) Hebe** is at opposition (mag. 8.4) in **Aquila** on July 17 (see chart on page 26).

The path of the Sun and the planets along the ecliptic in July.

Calendar for July

1	21:11	Last Quarter
2–Aug.14		α-Capricornid meteor shower
04	15:25	Uranus 2.1°N of Moon
04	19:45	Mercury at greatest elongation (21.6°W, mag. 0.4)
05	14:47	Moon at apogee (405,341 km)
05	22:27	Earth at aphelion (1.016729224 AU = 152,100,527 km)
06	23:27	Aldebaran 5.6°S of Moon
08	04:38	Mercury 3.8°S of Moon
10	01:17	New Moon
10	12:58	Pollux 3.2°N of Moon
12	09:08	Venus 3.3°S of Moon
12	10:10	Mars 3.8°S of Moon
3–Aug.24		Southern δ-Aquariid meteor shower
13	05:33	Regulus 4.9°S of Moon
13	07:00 *	Mars 0.5°S of Venus
6–Aug.23		Perseid meteor shower
17	04:33	Spica 6.4°S of Moon
17	10:11	First Quarter
17	11:29	Minor Planet (6) Hebe at opposition (mag. 8.4)
20	12:38	Antares 4.7°S of Moon
21	10:24	Moon at perigee (364,520 km)
21	19:00 *	Venus 1.2°N of Regulus
24	02:37	Full Moon
24	16:39	Saturn 3.8°N of Moon
26	01:21	Jupiter 4.2°N of Moon
27	17:44	Neptune 4.2°N of Moon
29	16:00 *	Mars 0.7°N of Regulus
30		α-Capricornid shower maximum
30		Southern δ-Aquariid shower maximum
1	13:16	Last Quarter

These objects are close together for an extended

Early morning 4:15 (BST)

Capella

Pleiades

Aldebaran

7

Elnath

8

Mercury

ENE

NE

10°

July 7–8 • In the early morning, shortly before sunrise, the narrow crescent Moon passes Aldebaran, Elnath and Mercury.

Evening 22:00 (BST)

Denebola

13

Algieba

12

Regulus

Venus

Mars

WNW

W

10°

11

July 11–13 • The Moon passes Venus and Mars and then enters the constellation of Leo, the Lion. Mars is still at magnitude 1.8, but will not be hard to find, because it is close to Venus.

Evening 22:00 (BST)

Sabik

Moon

Antares

S

10°

July 20 • The waxing gibbous Moon is due south, and in the company of Antares and Sabik

Evening 23:30 (BST)

Saturn

24

Jupiter

25

S

SSE

10°

July 24–25 • On July 24, the Moon is near Saturn, very low in southern sky. One day later it is close to Jupiter.

AQUARIUS

PEGASUS

Circlet

Great Square of Pegasus

Alpheratz

ANDROMEDA

PISCES

Hamal

ARIES

Andromeda Galaxy M31

NGC 752

TRIANGULUM

Algol

PERSEUS

LACERTA

Caph

Perseids

CEPHEUS

Double Cluster

CASSIOPEIA

The Kids

AURIGA

Deneb

Capella

CYGNUS

α-Aurigids

ZENITH

Polaris

CAMELOPARDALIS

N

M57 *Ring Nebula*

LYRA

Vega

URSA MINOR

LYNX

DRACO

M13

Keystone

HERCULES

LEO MINOR

URSA MAJOR

Alphecca

CORONA BOREALIS

The Plough

OPHIUCHUS

SERPENS CAPUT

M3

BOÖTES

CANES VENATICI

Melotte 111

COMA BERENICES

Arcturus

LIBRA

VIRGO

W

E

ECLIPTIC

Pleiades

August 01   00:00 BST (GMT + 1hr)
August 15   23:00 BST (GMT + 1hr)

August – Looking North

Ursa Major is now the 'right way up' in the northwest, although some of the fainter stars in the south of the constellation are difficult to see. Beyond it, *Boötes* stands almost vertically in the west, but pale orange *Arcturus* is sinking towards the horizon. Higher in the sky, both *Corona Borealis* and *Hercules* are clearly visible.

In the northeast, *Capella* is clearly seen, but most of *Auriga* still remains below the horizon. Higher in the sky, *Perseus* is gradually coming into full view and, later in the night and later in the month, the beautiful *Pleiades* cluster rises above the northeastern horizon. Between Perseus and *Polaris* lies the faint and unremarkable constellation of *Camelopardalis*.

Higher still, both *Cassiopeia* and *Cepheus* are well placed for observation, despite the fact that Cassiopeia is completely immersed in the band of the Milky Way, as is the 'base' of Cepheus. *Pegasus* and *Andromeda* are now well above the eastern horizon and, below them, the constellation of *Pisces* is climbing into view. Two of the stars in the *Summer Triangle, Deneb* and *Vega*, are close to the zenith high overhead.

Meteors

August is the month when one of the best meteor showers of the year occurs: the *Perseids*. This is a long shower, generally beginning about July 16 and continuing until around August 23, with a maximum in 2021 on August 12–13, when the rate may reach as high as 100 meteors per hour (and on rare occasions, even higher). In 2021, maximum is just after New Moon, so conditions are favourable. The Perseids are debris from Comet 109P/Swift-Tuttle (the Great Comet of 1862). Perseid meteors are fast and many of the brighter ones leave persistent trains. Some bright fireballs also occur during the shower.

A brilliant Perseid fireball, streaking alongside the Great Rift in the Milky Way, photographed in 2012 by Jens Hackmann from near Weikersheim in Germany. Four additional, fainter Perseids are also visible in the image.

August – Looking South

The whole stretch of the summer Milky Way stretches across the sky in the south, from **Cygnus**, high in the sky near the zenith, past **Aquila**, with bright **Altair** (α Aquilae), to part of the constellation of **Sagittarius** close to the horizon, where the pattern of stars known as the 'Teapot' may be just visible. This area contains many nebulae and both open and globular clusters. Between **Albireo** (β Cygni) and Altair lie the two small constellations of **Vulpecula** and **Sagitta**, with the latter easier to distinguish (because of its shape) from the clouds of the Milky Way. Between Sagitta and **Pegasus** to the east lie the highly distinctive five stars that form the tiny constellation of **Delphinus** (again, one of the few constellations that actually bear some resemblance to the creatures after which they are named). Below Aquila, mainly in the star clouds of the Milky Way, lies **Scutum**, most famous for the bright open cluster, **M11** or the 'Wild Duck Cluster', readily visible in binoculars. To the southeast of Aquila lie the two zodiacal constellations of **Capricornus** and **Aquarius**.

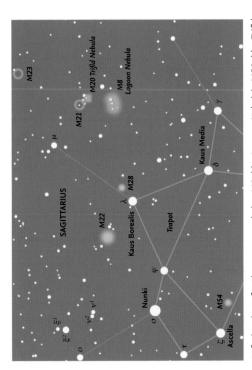

A finder chart for the gaseous nebulae M8 (the Lagoon Nebula), M20 (the Trifid Nebula) and the globular cluster M22, all in Sagittarius. Clusters M21, M23 (open) and M28 (globular) are faint. The chart shows all stars brighter than magnitude 7.5.

The Moon's phases for August

August – Moon and Planets

The Moon

The Moon passes north of **Aldebaran** on August 3. On August 6, the waning crescent is between **Castor** (α Geminorum) and **Alhena** (γ Geminorum), later that day it is 3.1° south of **Pollux**. On August 10, just after New Moon (on August 8), the hair-thin waxing crescent passes **Mars**, low in the evening sky, and the next day 4.3° north of **Venus**. On August 13, the Moon passes **Spica** in **Virgo**, and is 4.5° north of **Antares** in **Scorpius** on August 16. On August 20, the Moon is 3.7° south of **Saturn** and the next day 4.0° south of **Jupiter**. It passes **Aldebaran** in **Taurus** on August 30.

The planets

Mercury is at superior conjunction on the far side of the Sun on August 1. **Venus** is in **Virgo**, but too low to be readily visible except briefly in the evening twilight. **Mars** is in **Leo**, initially close to **Regulus**, but moving eastward toward **Virgo**, and very low in the sky. **Jupiter** (mag. -2.8 to -2.9) is in **Capricornus** and comes to opposition on August 20. **Saturn** (mag. 0.2) is at opposition in **Capricornus** on August 2. **Uranus** (mag. 5.8–5.7) in **Aries** begins retrograde motion on August 20. **Neptune** (mag. 7.9) remains in **Aquarius**.

The path of the Sun and the planets along the ecliptic in August.

Calendar for August

01	00:29	Uranus 1.8°N of Moon
01	14:07	Mercury at superior conjunction
02	06:14	Saturn at opposition (mag. 0.2)
02	07:35	Moon at apogee (404,410 km)
03	06:53	Aldebaran 5.7°S of Moon
06	20:14	Pollux 3.1°N of Moon
08	13:50	New Moon
09	03:19	Mercury 3.4°S of Moon
09	12:04	Regulus 4.8°S of Moon
10	00:41	Mars 4.3°S of Moon
11	06:59	Venus 4.3°S of Moon
12–13		Perseid shower maximum
13	10:03	Spica 6.1°S of Moon
15	15:20	First Quarter
16	19:06	Antares 4.5°S of Moon
17	09:16	Moon at perigee (369,124 km)
19	04:00 *	Mercury 0.1°S of Mars
20	00:28	Jupiter at opposition (mag. –2.9)
22	22:15	Saturn 3.7°N of Moon
22	04:56	Jupiter 4.0°N of Moon
22	12:02	Full Moon
24	01:55	Neptune 4.0°N of Moon
28–Sep.05		α-Aurigid meteor shower
28	08:57	Uranus 1.5°N of Moon
30	02:22	Moon at apogee (404,100 km)
30	07:13	Last Quarter
30	14:55	Aldebaran 6.0°S of Moon

* These objects are close together for an extended period around this time.

Early morning 5:00 (BST)

August 6–7 • Shortly before sunrise, on August 6, the narrow crescent Moon is between Castor and Alhena. One day later it is below Pollux.

Evening 21:00 (BST)

August 10–11 • The waxing, but still very narrow, crescent Moon passes Venus low in the west. Denebola is to be found a little higher.

Evening 21:00 (BST)

August 16 • Antares is less than five degrees below the Moon. Sabik is about eight degrees higher and more to the south.

Evening 23:30 (BST)

August 20–21 • The Moon is south of Saturn on August 20 and almost due south. One day later it is approaching Jupiter.

September   Looking North

September – Looking North

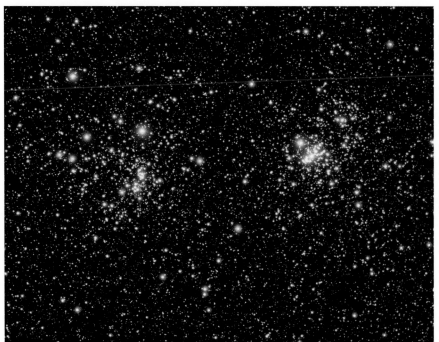

The twin open clusters, known as the Double Cluster, in Perseus (more formally called h and χ Persei) are close to the main portion of the Milky Way.

The (northern) autumnal equinox occurs on September 22, when the Sun moves south of the equator in Virgo.

Ursa Major is now low in the north and to the northwest **Arcturus** and much of **Boötes** sink below the horizon later in the night and later in the month. In the northeast, **Auriga** is beginning to climb higher in the sky. Later in the month, **Taurus**, with orange **Aldebaran** (α Tauri), and even **Gemini**, with **Castor** and **Pollux**, become visible in the east and northeast. Due east, **Andromeda** is now clearly visible, with the small constellations of **Triangulum** and **Aries** (the latter a zodiacal constellation) directly below it. Practically the whole of the northern Milky Way is visible, arching across the sky, both in the north and in the south. It is not particularly clear in Auriga, or even **Perseus**, but in **Cassiopeia** and on towards **Cygnus** the clouds of stars become easier to see. The **Double Cluster** in Perseus is well placed for observation. Cepheus is 'upside-down' near the zenith, and the head of **Draco** and **Hercules** (with the globular cluster **M13**), beyond it are well placed for observation.

Meteors

After the major Perseid shower in August, there is very little shower activity in September. One minor, but very extended, shower, known as the **α-Aurigids**, tends to have two peaks of activity. The principal peak occurs on September 1. In 2021, the Moon is a waning crescent, so conditions are reasonably favourable. At maximum, however, the hourly rate hardly reaches 10 meteors per hour, although the meteors are bright and relatively easy to photograph. Activity from this shower may even extend into October. The **Southern Taurid** shower begins this month (on September 10) and, although rates are low, often produces very bright fireballs. This is a very long shower, lasting until about November 20. As a slight compensation for the lack of shower activity, however, in September the number of sporadic meteors reaches its highest rate at any time during the year.

September 01 00:00 BST (GMT + 1hr)
September 15 23:00 BST (GMT + 1hr)

September — Looking South

September – Looking South

The **Summer Triangle** is now high in the southwest, with the Great Square of **Pegasus** high in the southeast. Below Pegasus are the two zodiacal constellations of **Capricornus** and **Aquarius**. In what is otherwise an unremarkable constellation, **Algedi** (α Capricorni) is actually a visual binary, with the two stars (α¹ Cap and α² Cap) readily seen with the naked eye. **Dabih** (β Capricorni), just to the south, is also a double star, and the components are relatively easy to separate with binoculars. In Aquarius, just to the east of **Sadalmelik** (α Aquarii) there is a tiny letter 'Y', known as the 'Water Jar', a small asterism consisting of four stars, resembling a sparsely populated area of the sky with just one bright star in the constellation of **Piscis Austrinus**. In classical illustrations, water is shown flowing from the 'Water Jar' towards bright **Fomalhaut** (α Piscis Austrini).

Another zodiacal constellation, **Pisces**, is now clearly visible to the east of Aquarius. Although faint, there is a distinctive asterism of stars, known as the 'Circlet', south of the Great Square and another line of faint stars to the east of Pegasus. Still farther down towards the horizon

The zodiacal constellation of Capricornus, photographed in 2009. The brilliant object is the planet Jupiter, which will again be in the constellation for part of 2021.

is the constellation of **Cetus**, with the famous variable star **Mira** (ο Ceti) at its centre. When Mira is at maximum brightness (around mag. 3.5) it is clearly visible to the naked eye, but it disappears as it fades towards minimum (about mag. 9.5 or less). There is a finder chart for Mira on page 97.

The Moon's phases for September

September – Moon and Planets

The Moon

On September 3, the Moon passes 3.0° south of **Pollux** in **Gemini**. On September 5, the Moon is 4.8° north of **Regulus** in the morning sky. On September 9, the young crescent Moon is 5.9° north of **Spica**, but the star will be difficult to detect in the evening twilight. The next day, the Moon passes 4.1° north of **Venus**. On September 17–18, the Moon passes south of first **Saturn**, and then **Jupiter** (both in **Capricornus**). On September 25, the Moon passes south of the **Pleiades** and then, on September 26, is 6.2° north of **Aldebaran** in **Taurus**. On September 30, the waning crescent Moon is 2.8° south of **Pollux** in **Gemini**.

The planets

Mercury is at greatest eastern elongation 26.8° on September 14, but only mag. 0.1. Initially, **Venus** is close to **Spica** in **Virgo** but then moves into **Libra**. Generally, it is in the evening twilight, but becomes slightly higher towards the end of the month. **Mars** is too close to the Sun to be seen. **Jupiter** (mag. -2.9 to -2.7) is still retrograding slowly in **Capricornus**, close to **Deneb Algedi** (δ Capricorni). **Saturn** (mag. 0.3–0.5) is also retrograding extremely slowly in **Capricornus**. **Uranus** (mag. 5.7) remains in **Aries** and **Neptune** (mag. 7.8) comes to opposition in **Aquarius** on September 14 (see the chart on page 25). Minor planet **(2) Pallas** (mag. 8.5) is at opposition in western **Pisces** on September 11 (see chart on page 27).

The path of the Sun and the planets along the ecliptic in September.

Calendar for September

These objects are close together for an extended period around this time.

Evening 19:45 (BST)

September 9 • The Moon, Venus and Spica. The Sun is less than four degrees below the horizon, so Spica will not be easy to detect.

Evening 20:00 (BST)

September 16–18 • The waxing gibbous Moon passes Saturn (mag. 0.9) and Jupiter (mag. –2.8), low in the southeastern sky.

Evening 23:00 (BST)

September 25–26 • The waning gibbous Moon passes the Pleiades and Aldebaran. The brightest member of the Pleiades cluster is Alcyone (mag. 2.9).

Morning 6:00 (BST)

September 30 • In the early morning, the Moon is in the company of Castor and Pollux, high in the southeast. Alhena and Procyon are nearby.

October 01   00:00 BST (GMT + 1hr)

October 15   23:00 BST (GMT + 1hr)

November 01   21:00 GMT

October Looking North

October – Looking North

Ursa Major is grazing the horizon in the north, while high overhead are the constellations of *Cepheus*, *Cassiopeia* and *Perseus*, with the Milky Way between Cepheus and Cassiopeia at the zenith. *Auriga* is now clearly visible in the east, as is *Taurus* with the *Pleiades*, *Hyades* and orange *Aldebaran*. Also in the east, *Orion* and *Gemini* are starting to rise clear of the horizon.

The constellations of *Boötes* and *Corona Borealis* are now essentially lost to view in the northwest, and *Hercules* is also descending towards the western horizon. The three stars of the Summer Triangle are still clearly visible, although *Aquila* and *Altair* are beginning to approach the horizon in the west. Towards the end of the month (October 31) Summer Time ends in Europe, with Britain reverting to Greenwich Mean Time and Europe to Central European Time.

Meteors

The *Orionids* are the major, fairly reliable meteor shower active in October. Like the May *η-Aquariid* shower, the Orionids are associated with Comet 1P/Halley. During this second pass through the stream of particles from the comet, slightly fewer meteors are seen than in May, but conditions are more favourable for northern observers. In both showers the meteors are very fast, and many leave persistent trains. Although the Orionid maximum is quoted as October 21, in fact there is a very broad maximum, lasting about a week roughly centred on that date, with hourly rates around 25. Occasionally, rates are higher (50–70 per hour). In 2021, Full Moon is on October 20, so there will be considerable interference from moonlight.

The faint shower of the *Southern Taurids* (often with bright fireballs) peaks on October 10. The Southern Taurid maximum occurs when the Moon is a waxing crescent, so conditions are more favourable than

The constellation of Perseus is not only the location of the radiant of the Perseid meteor shower in August, but is also well known for the pair of open clusters, called the Double Cluster (near the top edge of the image), close to the border with Cassiopeia, and also for Algol (β Persei), the famous variable star (near the centre of the photograph). The Pleiades, an open cluster in Taurus, is close to the bottom edge of the image.

for the Orionids. Towards the end of the month (around October 20), another shower (the Northern Taurids) begins to show activity, which peaks early in November. The parent comet for both Taurid showers is Comet 2P/Encke. The meteors in both Taurid streams are relatively slow and bright.

October – Looking South

The Great Square of **Pegasus** dominates the southern sky, framed by the two chains of stars that form the constellation of **Pisces**, together with **Alrescha** (α Piscium) at the point where the two lines of stars join. Also clearly visible is the constellation of **Cetus**, below Pegasus and Pisces. Although **Capricornus** is beginning to disappear, **Aquarius** to its east is well placed in the south, with solitary **Fomalhaut** and the constellation of **Piscis Austrinus** beneath it, close to the horizon.

The main band of the Milky Way and the Great Rift runs down from **Cygnus**, through **Vulpecula**, **Sagitta** and **Aquila** towards the western horizon. **Delphinus** and the tiny, unremarkable constellation of **Equuleus** lie between the band of the Milky Way and Pegasus. **Andromeda** is clearly visible high in the sky to the southeast, with the small constellation of **Triangulum** and the zodiacal constellation of **Aries** below it. **Perseus** is high in the east, and by now the **Pleiades** and **Taurus** are well clear of the horizon. Later in the night, and later in the month, **Orion** rises in the east, a sign that the autumn season has arrived and of the steady approach of winter.

The Moon's phases for October

The constellation of Aquarius is one of the constellations that is visible in late summer and early autumn. The four stars forming the 'Y'-shape of the 'Water Jar' may be seen to the east of Sadalmelik (α Aquarii), the brightest star (top centre).

October – Moon and Planets

The Moon

On October 3, the waning crescent Moon passes between **Regulus** (α Leonis) and **Algieba** (γ Leonis) in the early morning sky. On October 9, the Moon is 2.9° north of **Venus**, and it passes 4.0° north of **Antares** on October 10, both low in the evening sky. On October 14, the Moon passes 3.9° south of **Saturn** and, the next day, 4.1° south of **Jupiter**. The waning gibbous Moon is 6.4° north of **Aldebaran** on October 24. On October 27, the Moon passes 3.0° south of **Pollux**, and on October 30 passes 5.1° north of **Regulus** in **Leo**.

The planets

Mercury passes inferior conjunction on October 9 and is mag. -0.6 at greatest western elongation (18.4°) on October 25. **Venus** is close to **Antares** for several days low in the eastern sky, passing 1.5° due north of the star on October 16. It is very bright (mag. -4.5) when at its greatest possible eastern elongation (47°) on October 29. **Mars** is at superior conjunction on October 8. **Jupiter** (mag. -2.5 to -2.7) is initially retrograding in **Capricornus** but begins direct motion on October 30. **Saturn** (mag. 0.5–0.6), also in **Capricornus**, reverts to direct motion on October 19. **Uranus** (mag. 5.7) is retrograding in **Aries**. **Neptune** (mag. 7.8) continues retrograde motion in **Aquarius**.

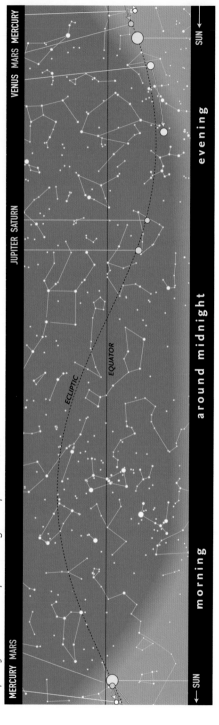

The path of the Sun and the planets along the ecliptic in October.

Date	Time	Event
01–Nov.06		Orionid meteor shower
03	05:42	Regulus 5.0°S of Moon
06	09:40	Mars 3.6°S of Moon
06	11:05	New Moon
6	17:39	Mercury 6.9°S of Moon
07–11		Draconid meteor shower
07	01:13	Spica 5.8°S of Moon
08	04:01	Mars in conjunction with the Sun
08	17:28	Moon at perigee (363,386 km)
08–09		Draconid shower maximum
09	16:18	Mercury at inferior conjunction
09	18:36	Venus 2.9°S of Moon
0		Southern Taurid shower maximum
0	06:58	Antares 4.0°S of Moon
3	03:25	First Quarter
4	07:08	Saturn 3.9°N of Moon
5	10:03	Jupiter 4.1°N of Moon
6	14:00 *	Venus 1.5°N of Antares
7	13:58	Neptune 4.1°N of Moon
0	06:00 *	Mars 2.8°N of Spica
0	14:57	Full Moon
0–Dec.10		Northern Taurid meteor shower
21	21:40	Uranus 1.3°N of Moon
24	06:17	Aldebaran 6.4°S of Moon
4	15:28	Moon at apogee (405,615 km)
25	05:30	Mercury at greatest elongation (18.4°W, mag. −0.6)
7	21:15	Pollux 3.0°N of Moon
8	20:05	Last Quarter
29	20:52	Venus at greatest elongation (47.0°E, mag. −4.5)
0	15:04	Regulus 5.1°S of Moon
1		European Daylight Saving Time ends (UK – Summer Time)

These objects are close together for an extended

Morning 6:00 (BST)

October 3 • In the early morning, the waning crescent Moon is between Regulus and Algieba. Denebola is closer to the horizon and more to the northeast.

Evening 18:45 (BST)

October 9–10 • Shortly after sunset, the crescent Moon passes Venus and Antares, very low in the southwest. On October 10, Sabik is ten degrees above the Moon.

Evening 19:00 (BST)

October 14 • The Moon in the company of Saturn and Jupiter in the south-southeast.

Evening 18:30 (BST)

October 16 • Antares is 1.5° below the much brighter Venus

Evening 23:30 (BST)

October 27 • The waning gibbous Moon lines up with

November – Looking North

November – Looking North

Most of **Aquila** has now disappeared below the horizon, but two of the stars of the Summer Triangle, **Vega** in **Lyra** and **Deneb** in **Cygnus**, are still clearly visible in the west. The head of **Draco** is now low in the northwest and only a small portion of **Hercules** remains above the horizon. The southernmost stars of **Ursa Major** are now coming into view. The Milky Way arches overhead, with the denser star clouds in the west and the less heavily populated region through **Auriga** and **Monoceros** in the east. High overhead, **Cassiopeia** is near the zenith and **Cepheus** has swung round to the northwest, while Auriga is now high in the northeast. **Gemini**, with **Castor** and **Pollux**, is well clear of the eastern horizon, and even **Procyon** (α Canis Minoris) is just climbing into view almost due east.

Meteors

The **Northern Taurid** shower, which began in mid-October, reaches maximum – although with just a low rate of about five meteors per hour – on November 12. First Quarter is on November 11, so conditions are reasonably favourable. The shower gradually trails off, ending around December 10. There is an apparent 7-year periodicity in fireball activity, but 2021 is unlikely to be a peak year. Far more striking, however, are the **Leonids**, which have a relatively short period of activity (November 5–29), with maximum on November 17–18. This shower is associated with Comet 55P/Tempel-Tuttle and has shown extraordinary activity on various occasions with many thousands of meteors per hour. High rates were seen in 1999, 2001 and 2002 (reaching about 3000 meteors per hour) but have fallen dramatically since then. The rate in 2021 is likely to be about 15 per hour. These meteors are the fastest shower meteors recorded (about 70 km per second) and often leave persistent trains. The shower is very rich in faint meteors. In 2021, maximum is just before Full Moon (on November 19), so conditions are very unfavourable.

The constellation of Auriga, with brilliant Capella (mag. 0.08), which, although appearing as a single star, is actually a quadruple system, consisting of a pair of yellow giant stars, gravitationally bound to a more distant pair of red dwarfs.

November Looking South

November – Looking South

Orion has now risen above the eastern horizon, and part of the long, straggling constellation of **Eridanus** (which begins near **Rigel**) is visible to the west of Orion. Higher in the sky, **Taurus**, with the **Pleiades** cluster, and orange **Aldebaran** are now easy to observe. To their west, both **Pisces** and **Cetus** are close to the meridian. The famous long-period variable star, **Mira** (o Ceti), with a typical range of magnitude 3.4 to 9.8, is favourably placed for observation. In the southwest, **Capricornus** has slipped below the horizon, but **Aquarius** remains visible. Even farther west, **Altair** may be seen early in the night, but most of **Aquila** has already disappeared from view. **Delphinus**, together with **Sagitta** and **Vulpecula** in the Milky Way, will soon vanish for another year. Both **Pegasus** and **Andromeda** are easy to see, and one of the lines of stars that make up Andromeda finishes close to the zenith, which is also close to one of the outlying stars of **Perseus**, high in the east.

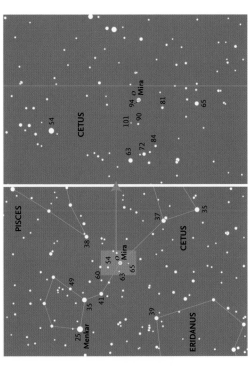

Finder and comparison charts for Mira (o Ceti). The chart on the left shows all stars brighter than magnitude 6.5. The chart on the right shows stars down to magnitude 10.0. The comparison star magnitudes are shown without the decimal point.

The Moon's phases for November

November – Moon and Planets

The Moon

On November 3, the extremely narrow waning crescent Moon (one day before New Moon) passes close to **Mercury** and **Spica**. On November 7–8, the young waxing crescent may be glimpsed low in the evening sky, close to **Venus**. On November 10, the Moon passes 4.1° south of **Saturn** and then on November 11, 4.4° south of **Jupiter**. On November 19, at Full Moon, there is a partial lunar eclipse. Just the start of this eclipse is visible from the UK, but it is fully visible from North and South America, the Pacific region, Australia and most of Asia. The next day (November 20), the Moon is north of **Aldebaran**. On November 24 it is 2.5° south of **Pollux**, and then on November 26, 5.2° north of **Regulus** in **Leo**. By November 30, it is north of **Spica** in **Virgo**.

The planets

Mercury is too close to the Sun to be visible during the month. It is at superior conjunction on November 29. **Venus** is low in **Sagittarius**. It passes south of **Nunki** (σ Sagattarii) on November 19. **Mars** (mag. 1.6) is in **Virgo**, moving into **Libra**, and may be glimpsed in the morning twilight. **Jupiter** (mag. -2.5 to -2.3) is in **Capricornus**, near **Deneb Algedi** (δ Capricorni). **Saturn** (mag. 0.6–0.7) is also in **Capricornus**. **Uranus** (mag. 5.7) is in **Aries** and comes to opposition on November 4. **Neptune** (mag. 7.8) continues slow retrograde motion in **Aquarius**. Dwarf planet **(1) Ceres** is at opposition at mag. 7.0 in **Taurus**, not that far from **Aldebaran**, on November 27 (see the chart on page 27).

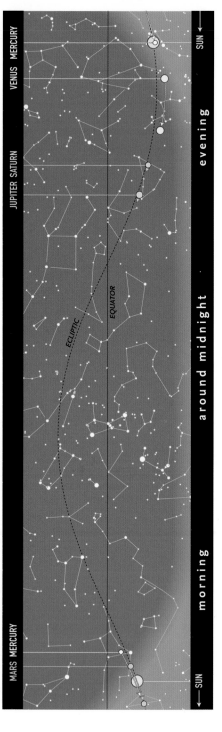

The path of the Sun and the planets along the ecliptic in November.

1	02:00 *	Mercury 4.4°N of Spica
3	11:49	Spica 5.8°S of Moon
3	18:39	Mercury 1.2°S of Moon
4	04:36	Mars 2.3°S of Moon
4	21:15	New Moon
4	23:58	Uranus at opposition (mag. 5.7)
5	22:18	Moon at perigee (358,844 km)
5–29		Leonid meteor shower
6	15:58	Antares 3.9°S of Moon
7		North American Daylight Saving Time ends
8	05:21	Venus 1.1°S of Moon
0	04:00 *	Mercury 1.1°N of Mars
0	14:24	Saturn 4.1°N of Moon
1	12:46	First Quarter
1	17:16	Jupiter 4.4°N of Moon
2		Northern Taurid shower maximum
3	18:37	Neptune 4.2°N of Moon
7–18		Leonid shower maximum
8	01:51	Uranus 1.5°N of Moon
9	08:57	Full Moon
9	09:27	Partial lunar eclipse (Americas, Pacific, Australia, Asia)
0	12:53	Aldebaran 6.4°S of Moon
1	02:13	Moon at apogee (406,279 km)
4	03:58	Pollux 2.5°N of Moon
6	23:00	Regulus 5.2°S of Moon
7	03:50	Dwarf planet (1) Ceres at opposition (mag. 7.0)
7	12:28	Last Quarter
9	04:39	Mercury at superior conjunction
0	22:35	Spica 5.9°S of Moon

*These objects are close together for an extended period around this time.

Morning 6:15

ESE

Mercury • Spica

November 1 • *Before sunrise, Mercury and Spica are low in the east-southeastern sky.*

Morning 6:30

Moon

Mercury • Spica

ESE

November 3 • *Mercury and Spica are joined by the narrow crescent Moon.*

Evening 17:00

Nunki •

Venus

8

SSW

November 7–8 • *The waxing crescent Moon passes Venus, shortly after sunset. Nunki is a little farther south.*

Evening 17:00

Nunki
20 19 18
Venus

SSW

November 18–20 • *Venus passes Nunki, low in the south-southwest. (Note that the scale of the illustration is different from the others.)*

Morning 7:00

45°

Castor
Pollux
Moon

Procyon

Alhena

W

W·SW

November 24 • *The Moon lines up with Castor and Pollux, halfway between the horizon and the zenith. Procyon and Alhena are about twenty degrees lower.*

December Looking North

December – Looking North

Ursa Major has now swung around and is starting to 'climb' in the east. The fainter stars in the southern part of the constellation are now fully in view. The other bear, *Ursa Minor*, 'hangs' below *Polaris* in the north. Directly above it is the faint constellation of *Camelopardalis*, with the other inconspicuous circumpolar constellation, *Lynx*, to its east. *Vega* (α Lyrae) is skimming the horizon in the northwest, but *Deneb* (α Cygni) and most of *Cygnus* remain visible farther west. In the east, *Regulus* (α Leonis) and the constellation of *Leo* are beginning to rise above the horizon. *Cancer* stands high in the east, with *Gemini* even higher in the sky. *Perseus* is at the zenith, with *Auriga* and *Capella* between it and Gemini. Because it is so high in the sky, now is a good time to examine the star clouds of the fainter portion of the Milky Way, between *Cassiopeia* in the west to Gemini and *Orion* in the east.

Meteors

There is one significant meteor shower in December (the last major shower of the year). This is the *Geminid* shower, which is visible over the period December 3–16 and comes to maximum on December 14, when the Moon is waxing gibbous so conditions are not wonderful. It is one of the most active showers of the year, and in some years is the strongest, with a peak rate of around 100 meteors per hour. It is the one major shower that shows good activity before midnight. The meteors have been found to have a much higher density than other meteors (which are derived from cometary material). It was eventually established that the Geminids and the asteroid Phaeton had similar orbits. So the Geminids are assumed to consist of denser, rocky material. They are slower than most other meteors and often appear to last longer. The brightest often break up into numerous luminous fragments that follow similar paths across the sky. There is a second shower: the *Ursids*, active December 17–26, peaking on December 22–23,

with a rate at maximum of 5–10, occasionally rising to 25 per hour. Maximum in 2021 is when the Moon is waning gibbous, so conditions for this shower are unfavourable. The parent body is Comet 8P/Tuttle.

The constellation of Cassiopeia is a familiar sight among the northern circumpolar constellations. It is always above the horizon, on the opposite side of Polaris (the North Star) to the equally well-known asterism of the seven stars of the Plough.

December 01   23:00 GMT
December 15   22:00 GMT
January 01   21:00 GMT

December – Looking South

December – Looking South

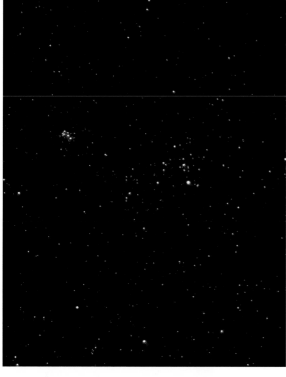

The fine open cluster of the **Pleiades** is due south around 22:00, with the **Hyades** cluster, **Aldebaran** and the rest of **Taurus** clearly visible to the east. **Auriga** (with **Capella**) and **Gemini** (with **Castor** and **Pollux**) are both well-placed for observation. **Orion** has made a welcome return to the winter sky, and both **Canis Minor** (with **Procyon**) and **Canis Major** (with **Sirius**, the brightest star in the sky) are now well above the horizon. The small, poorly known constellation of **Lepus** lies to the south of Orion. In the west, **Aquarius** has now disappeared, and **Cetus** is becoming lower, but **Pisces** is still easily seen, as are the constellations of **Aries**, **Triangulum** and **Andromeda** above it. The Great Square of **Pegasus** is starting to plunge down towards the western horizon, and because of its orientation on the sky appears more like a large diamond, standing on one point, than a square.

The constellation of Taurus contains two contrasting open clusters: the compact Pleiades, with its striking blue-white stars, and the more scattered, 'V'-shaped Hyades, which are much closer to us. Orange Aldebaran (α Tauri) is not related to the Hyades, but lies between it and the Earth.

The Moon's phases for December

		New Moon				
01	02	03	04 07:43	05	06	07
Day 27	Day 28	Day 29	Day 1	Day 2	Day 3	Day 4

			First Quarter			
08	09	10	11 01:36	12	13	14	15	16
Day 5	Day 6	Day 7	Day 8	Day 9	Day 10	Day 11	Day 12	Day 13

	Full Moon						Last Quarter	
17	18	19 04:35	20	21	22	23	24	25	26	27 02:24	28
Day 14	Day 15	Day 16	Day 17	Day 18	Day 19	Day 20	Day 21	Day 22	Day 23	Day 24	Day 25	Day 26	Day 27	Day 28

29	30	31
Day 26	Day 27	Day 28

December – Moon and Planets

The Moon

On December 4, at New Moon, there is a total solar eclipse, visible from Antarctica only. That day the Moon is at perigee (356,794 km), which is the closest to Earth in 2021, it also passes 3.9° north of *Antares* in *Scorpius*. On December 7 to 9, in the evening sky, the young waxing crescent Moon passes, in succession, *Venus* (December 7), *Saturn* (December 8) and *Jupiter* (December 9). On December 17, nearing Full, the Moon is 6.4° north of *Aldebaran*. On December 21, waning gibbous, it is 3.0° south of *Pollux* in *Gemini*. On December 24, it passes 5.1° north of *Regulus*. On December 31, in the morning sky, the waning crescent Moon is close to *Mars* and *Antares* and passes between the two.

The planets

Mercury is initially too close to the Sun to be visible, where it was actually occulted by the Moon on November 3. Towards the end of the month it moves into the evening twilight and may be glimpsed, low in the sky, when it is close to Venus. *Venus* is in *Sagittarius* but close to the Sun. It may be glimpsed for a short period in the evening sky at the end of the month. *Mars* begins the month in *Libra*, but soon becomes lost near the Sun. *Jupiter* (mag. -2.3 to -2.1) is in *Capricornus* and *Aquarius*, moving eastwards, and is visible in the evening sky. *Saturn* (mag. 0.7) is also in *Capricornus*, with slow direct motion, but closer to the horizon than Jupiter. *Uranus* (mag. 5.7) is slowly retrograding in *Aries*. *Neptune* (mag. 7.8) is in *Aquarius* and resumes direct motion on December 4.

The path of the Sun and the planets along the ecliptic in December.

Calendar for December

* These objects are close together for an extended period around this time.

Evening 17:00

December 6–8 • The waxing crescent Moon passes Venus and Saturn, low in the south-southwest. One day later (December 9) it has passed Jupiter as well.

Morning 7:00

December 24 • The Moon is between Regulus and Algieba, high in the south-southwest. Denebola is nearby.

Evening 16:30

December 29 • After sunset, Venus and Mercury are close together, low in the southwest. Saturn may be found a little higher and farther south.

Morning 7:30

December 31 • The crescent Moon in the company of Mars and its rival. (The name Antares means 'Rival of Mars'.) Sabik lines up with Mars and Antares.

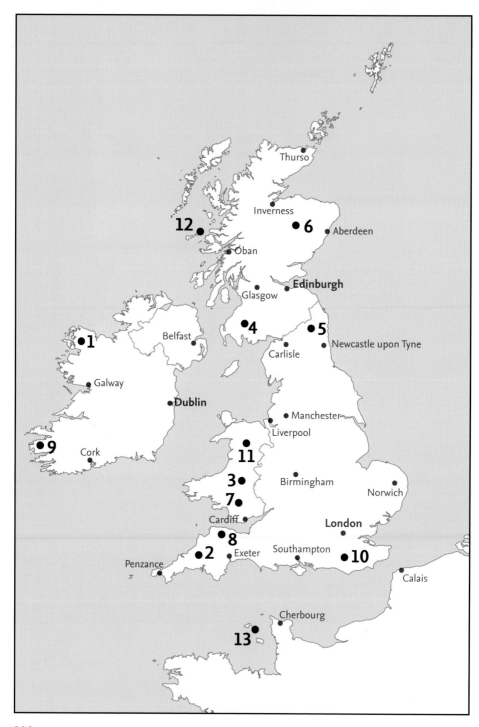

Dark Sky Sites

International Dark-Sky Association Sites

The *International Dark-Sky Association* (IDA) recognizes various categories of sites that offer areas where the sky is dark at night, free from light pollution and particularly suitable for astonomical observing. A number of sites in Great Britain and Ireland have been given specific recognition and are shown on the map. These are:

1   *Ballycroy National Park and Wild Nephin Wilderness*

2   *Bodmin Moor Dark Sky Landscape*

3   *Elan Valley Estate*

4   *Galloway Forest Park*

5   *Northumberland National Park and Kielder Water & Forest Park*

6   *Tomintoul and Glenlivet – Cairngorms*

7   *Brecon Beacons National Park*

8   *Exmoor National Park*

9   *Kerry*

10 *Moore's Reserve – South Downs National Park*

11 *Snowdonia National Park*

12 *The island of Coll (Inner Hebrides, Scotland)*

13 *The island of Sark (Channel Islands)*

Details of these sites and web links may be found at the IDA website: https://www.darksky.org/ Many of these sites have major observatories or other facilities available for public observing (often at specific dates or times).

Dark Sky Discovery Sites

In Britain there is also the *Dark Sky Discovery* organisation. This gives recognition to smaller sites, again free from immediate light pollution, that are open to observing at any time. Some sites are used for specific, public observing sessions. A full listing of sites is at:

https://www.darkskydiscovery.org.uk/

but specific events are publicized locally.

Glossary and Tables

aphelion	The point on an orbit that is farthest from the Sun.
apogee	The point on its orbit at which the Moon is farthest from the Earth.
appulse	The apparently close approach of two celestial objects; two planets, or a planet and star.
astronomical unit	(AU) The mean distance of the Earth from the Sun, 149,597,870 km.
celestial equator	The great circle on the celestial sphere that is in the same plane as the Earth's equator.
celestial sphere	The apparent sphere surrounding the Earth on which all celestial bodies (stars, planets, etc.) seem to be located.
conjunction	The point in time when two celestial objects have the same celestial longitude. In the case of the Sun and a planet, superior conjunction occurs when the planet lies on the far side of the Sun (as seen from Earth). For Mercury and Venus, inferior conjuction occurs when they pass between the Sun and the Earth.
direct motion	Motion from west to east on the sky.
ecliptic	The apparent path of the Sun across the sky throughout the year. Also: the plane of the Earth's orbit in space.
elongation	The point at which an inferior planet has the greatest angular distance from the Sun, as seen from Earth.
equinox	The two points during the year when night and day have equal duration. Also: the points on the sky at which the ecliptic intersects the celestial equator. The vernal (spring) equinox is of particular importance in astronomy.
gibbous	The stage in the sequence of phases at which the illumination of a body lies between half and full. In the case of the Moon, the term is applied to phases between First Quarter and Full, and between Full and Last Quarter.
inferior planet	Either of the planets Mercury or Venus, which have orbits inside that of the Earth.
magnitude	The brightness of a star, planet or other celestial body. It is a logarithmic scale, where larger numbers indicate fainter brightness. A difference of 5 in magnitude indicates a difference of 100 in actual brightness, thus a first-magnitude star is 100 times as bright as one of sixth magnitude.
meridian	The great circle passing through the North and South Poles of a body and the observer's position; or the corresponding great circle on the celestial sphere that passes through the North and South Celestial Poles and also through the observer's zenith.
nadir	The point on the celestial sphere directly beneath the observer's feet, opposite the zenith.
occultation	The disappearance of one celestial body behind another, such as when stars or planets are hidden behind the Moon.
opposition	The point on a superior planet's orbit at which it is directly opposite the Sun in the sky.
perigee	The point on its orbit at which the Moon is closest to the Earth.
perihelion	The point on an orbit that is closest to the Sun.
retrograde motion	Motion from east to west on the sky.
superior planet	A planet that has an orbit outside that of the Earth.
vernal equinox	The point at which the Sun, in its apparent motion along the ecliptic, crosses the celestial equator from south to north. Also known as the First Point of Aries.
zenith	The point directly above the observer's head.
zodiac	A band, stretching 8° on either side of the ecliptic, within which the Moon and planets appear to move. It consists of twelve equal areas, originally named after the constellation that once lay within it.

The Greek Alphabet

α	Alpha	ε	Epsilon	ι	Iota	ν	Nu	ρ	Rho	φ (φ)	Phi
β	Beta	ζ	Zeta	κ	Kappa	ξ	Xi	σ (ς)	Sigma	χ	Chi
γ	Gamma	η	Eta	λ	Lambda	ο	Omicron	τ	Tau	ψ	Psi
δ	Delta	θ (ϑ)	Theta	μ	Mu	π	Pi	υ	Upsilon	ω	Omega

The Constellations

There are 88 constellations covering the whole of the celestial sphere, but 24 of these in the southern hemisphere can never be seen (even in part) from the latitude of Britain and Ireland, so are omitted from this table. The names themselves are expressed in Latin, and the names of stars are frequently given by Greek letters followed by the genitive of the constellation name. The genitives and English names of the various constellations are included.

Name	Genitive	Abbr.	English name
Andromeda	Andromeda	And	Andromeda
Antlia	Antliae	Ant	Air Pump
Aquarius	Aquarii	Aqr	Water Bearer
Aquila	Aquilae	Aql	Eagle
Aries	Arietis	Ari	Ram
Auriga	Aurigae	Aur	Charioteer
Boötes	Boötis	Boo	Herdsman
Camelopardalis	Camelopardalis	Cam	Giraffe
Cancer	Cancri	Cnc	Crab
Canes Venatici	Canum Venaticorum	CVn	Hunting Dogs
Canis Major	Canis Majoris	CMa	Big Dog
Canis Minor	Canis Minoris	CMi	Little Dog
Capricornus	Capricorni	Cap	Sea Goat
Cassiopeia	Cassiopeiae	Cas	Cassiopeia
Centaurus	Centauri	Cen	Centaur
Cepheus	Cephei	Cep	Cepheus
Cetus	Ceti	Cet	Whale
Columba	Columbae	Col	Dove
Coma Berenices	Comae Berenices	Com	Berenice's Hair
Corona Australis	Coronae Australis	CrA	Southern Crown
Corona Borealis	Coronae Borealis	CrB	Northern Crown
Corvus	Corvi	Crv	Crow
Crater	Crateris	Crt	Cup
Cygnus	Cygni	Cyg	Swan
Delphinus	Delphini	Del	Dolphin
Draco	Draconis	Dra	Dragon
Equuleus	Equulei	Equ	Little Horse
Eridanus	Eridani	Eri	River Eridanus
Fornax	Fornacis	For	Furnace
Gemini	Geminorum	Gem	Twins
Hercules	Herculis	Her	Hercules
Hydra	Hydrae	Hya	Water Snake

Name	Genitive	Abbr.	English name
Lacerta	Lacertae	Lac	Lizard
Leo	Leonis	Leo	Lion
Leo Minor	Leonis Minoris	LMi	Little Lion
Lepus	Leporis	Lep	Hare
Libra	Librae	Lib	Scales
Lupus	Lupi	Lup	Wolf
Lynx	Lyncis	Lyn	Lynx
Lyra	Lyrae	Lyr	Lyre
Microscopium	Microscopii	Mic	Microscope
Monoceros	Monocerotis	Mon	Unicorn
Ophiuchus	Ophiuchi	Oph	Serpent Bearer
Orion	Orionis	Ori	Orion
Pegasus	Pegasi	Peg	Pegasus
Perseus	Persei	Per	Perseus
Pisces	Piscium	Psc	Fishes
Piscis Austrinus	Piscis Austrini	PsA	Southern Fish
Puppis	Puppis	Pup	Stern
Pyxis	Pyxidis	Pyx	Compass
Sagitta	Sagittae	Sge	Arrow
Sagittarius	Sagittarii	Sgr	Archer
Scorpius	Scorpii	Sco	Scorpion
Sculptor	Sculptoris	Scl	Sculptor
Scutum	Scuti	Sct	Shield
Serpens	Serpentis	Ser	Serpent
Sextans	Sextantis	Sex	Sextant
Taurus	Tauri	Tau	Bull
Triangulum	Trianguli	Tri	Triangle
Ursa Major	Ursae Majoris	UMa	Great Bear
Ursa Minor	Ursae Minoris	UMi	Lesser Bear
Vela	Velorum	Vel	Sails
Virgo	Virginis	Vir	Virgin
Vulpecula	Vulpeculae	Vul	Fox

Some common asterisms

Belt of Orion	δ, ε and ζ Orionis
Big Dipper	α, β, γ, δ, ε, ζ and η Ursae Majoris
Circlet	γ, θ, ι, λ and κ Piscium
Guards (or Guardians)	β and γ Ursae Minoris
Head of Cetus	α, γ, ξ², μ and λ Ceti
Head of Draco	β, γ, ξ and ν Draconis
Head of Hydra	δ, ε, ζ, η, ρ and σ Hydrae
Keystone	ε, ζ, η and π Herculis
Kids	ε, ζ and η Aurigae
Little Dipper	β, γ, η, ζ, ε, δ and α Ursae Minoris
Lozenge	= Head of Draco
Milk Dipper	ζ, γ, σ, φ and λ Sagittarii
Plough or Big Dipper	α, β, γ, δ, ε, ζ and η Ursae Majoris
Pointers	α and β Ursae Majoris
Sickle	α, η, γ, ζ, μ and ε Leonis
Square of Pegasus	α, β and γ Pegasi with α Andromedae
Sword of Orion	θ and ι Orionis
Teapot	γ, ε, δ, λ, φ, σ, τ and ζ Sagittarii
Wain (or Charles' Wain)	= Plough
Water Jar	γ, η, κ and ζ Aquarii
Y of Aquarius	= Water Jar

Acknowledgements

Denis Buczynski, Portmahomack, Ross-shire – p.32, 35 (Quadrantid fireball), p.65 (Noctilucent clouds)

Steve Edberg, La Cañada, California – pp.35, 43, 89, 91, 95, 101, 103 (constellation photographs)

Akira Fuji, Japan – p.21 (lunar eclipse)

Jens Hackmann, Bad Mergentheim, Germany – p.77 (Perseid fireball)

Bernhard Hubl – pp. 49, 53, 55, 67, 71, 85 (constellation photographs)

Damian Peach – p.29 (comet photos)

peresanz/Shutterstock – p.37 (Orion)

Jan Sandberg – p.24 (Jupiter & satellites)

Ken Sperber, California – p. 83 (Double Cluster)

Specialist editorial support was provided by Dr Emily Drabek-Maunder, Senior Manager of Public Astronomy and Dr Gregory Brown, Public Astronomy Officer at the Royal Observatory, part of Royal Museums Greewich.

Further Information

Books

Bone, Neil (1993), *Observer's Handbook: Meteors*, George Philip, London & Sky Publ. Corp., Cambridge, Mass.

Cook, J., ed. (1999), *The Hatfield Photographic Lunar Atlas*, Springer-Verlag, New York

Dunlop, Storm (1999), *Wild Guide to the Night Sky*, HarperCollins, London

Dunlop, Storm (2012), *Practical Astronomy*, 3rd edn, Philip's, London

Dunlop, Storm, Rükl, Antonin & Tirion, Wil (2005), *Collins Atlas of the Night Sky*, HarperCollins, London

Heifetz, Milton & Tirion, Wil (2017), *A Walk through the Heavens: A Guide to Stars and Consellations and their Legends*, 4th edn, Cambridge University Press, Cambridge

O'Meara, Stephen J. (2008), *Observing the Night Sky with Binoculars*, Cambridge University Press, Cambridge

Ridpath, Ian, ed. (2004), *Norton's Star Atlas*, 20th edn, Pi Press, New York

Ridpath, Ian, ed. (2003), *Oxford Dictionary of Astronomy*, 2nd edn, Oxford University Press, Oxford

Ridpath, Ian & Tirion, Wil (2004), *Collins Gem – Stars*, HarperCollins, London

Ridpath, Ian & Tirion, Wil (2011), *Collins Pocket Guide Stars and Planets*, 4th edn, HarperCollins, London

Ridpath, Ian & Tirion, Wil (2012), *Monthly Sky Guide*, 9th edn, Cambridge University Press

Rükl, Antonín (1990), *Hamlyn Atlas of the Moon*, Hamlyn, London & Astro Media Inc., Milwaukee

Rükl, Antonín (2004), *Atlas of the Moon*, Sky Publishing Corp., Cambridge, Mass.

Scagell, Robin (2000), *Philip's Stargazing with a Telescope*, George Philip, London

Tirion, Wil (2011), *Cambridge Star Atlas*, 4th edn, Cambridge University Press, Cambridge

Tirion, Wil & Sinnott, Roger (1999), *Sky Atlas 2000.0*, 2nd edn, Sky Publishing Corp., Cambridge, Mass. & Cambridge University Press, Cambridge

Journals

Astronomy, Astro Media Corp., 21027 Crossroads Circle, P.O. Box 1612, Waukesha, WI 53187-1612 USA. http://www.astronomy.com

Astronomy Now, Pole Star Publications, PO Box 175, Tonbridge, Kent TN10 4QX UK. http://www.astronomynow.com

Sky at Night Magazine, BBC publications, London. http://skyatnightmagazine.com

Sky & Telescope, Sky Publishing Corp., Cambridge, MA 02138-1200 USA. http://www.skyandtelescope.com/

Societies

British Astronomical Association, Burlington House, Piccadilly, London W1J 0DU. http://www.britastro.org/

The principal British organization for amateur astronomers (with some professional members), particularly for those interested in carrying out observational programmes. Its membership is, however, worldwide. It publishes fully refereed, scientific papers and other material in its well-regarded journal.

Federation of Astronomical Societies, Secretary: Ken Sheldon, Whitehaven, Maytree Road, Lower Moor, Pershore, Worcs. WR10 2NY. http://www.fedastro.org.uk/fas/

An organization that is able to provide contact information for local astronomical societies in the United Kingdom.

Royal Astronomical Society, Burlington House, Piccadilly, London W1J 0BQ. http://www.ras.org.uk/

The premier astronomical society, with membership primarily drawn from professionals and experienced amateurs. It has an exceptional library and is a designated centre for the retention of certain classes of astronomical data. Its publications are the standard medium for dissemination of astronomical research.

Society for Popular Astronomy, 36 Fairway, Keyworth, Nottingham NG12 5DU.

http://www.popastro.com/

A society for astronomical beginners of all ages, which concentrates on increasing members' understanding and enjoyment, but which does have some observational programmes. Its journal is entitled *Popular Astronomy*.

Software

Planetary, Stellar and Lunar Visibility, (Planetary and eclipse freeware): Alcyone Software, Germany.

http://www.alcyone.de

Redshift, Redshift-Live. http://www.redshift-live.com/en/

Starry Night & Starry Night Pro, Sienna Software Inc., Toronto, Canada. http://www.starrynight.com

Internet sources

There are numerous sites with information about all aspects of astronomy, and all of those have numerous links. Although many amateur sites are excellent, treat any statements and data with caution. The sites listed below offer accurate information. Please note that the URLs may change. If so, use a good search engine, such as Google, to locate the information source.

Information

Astronomical data (inc. eclipses) HM Nautical Almanac Office: http://astro.ukho.gov.uk

Auroral information Michigan Tech: http://www.geo.mtu.edu/weather/aurora/

Comets JPL Solar System Dynamics: http://ssd.jpl.nasa.gov/

American Meteor Society: http://amsmeteors.org/

Deep-sky objects Saguaro Astronomy Club Database: http://www.virtualcolony.com/sac/

Eclipses: NASA Eclipse Page: http://eclipse.gsfc.nasa.gov/eclipse.html

https://en.wikipedia.org/wiki/Solar_eclipse_of_June_10,_2021

Moon (inc. Atlas) Inconstant Moon: http://www.inconstantmoon.com/

Planets Planetary Fact Sheets: http://nssdc.gsfc.nasa.gov/planetary/planetfact.html

Satellites (inc. International Space Station)

Heavens Above: http://www.heavens-above.com/

Visual Satellite Observer: http://www.satobs.org/

Star Chart http://www.skyandtelescope.com/observing/interactive-sky-watching-tools/interactive-sky-chart/

What's Visible

Skyhound: http://www.skyhound.com/sh/skyhound.html

Skyview Cafe: http://www.skyviewcafe.com

Institutes and Organizations

European Space Agency: http://www.esa.int/

International Dark-Sky Association: http://www.darksky.org/

RASC Dark Sky: https://www.rasc.ca/dark-sky-site-designations

Jet Propulsion Laboratory: http://www.jpl.nasa.gov/

Lunar and Planetary Institute: http://www.lpi.usra.edu/

National Aeronautics and Space Administration: http://www.hq.nasa.gov/

Solar Data Analysis Center: http://umbra.gsfc.nasa.gov/

Space Telescope Science Institute: http://www.stsci.edu/